Henry Eduard Legler

A Moses of the Mormons

Henry Eduard Legler

A Moses of the Mormons

ISBN/EAN: 9783744725002

Printed in Europe, USA, Canada, Australia, Japan

Cover: Foto ©Lupo / pixelio.de

More available books at **www.hansebooks.com**

A MOSES OF THE MORMONS

Strang's City of Refuge and Island Kingdom

By HENRY E. LEGLER

A MOSES OF THE MORMONS.

STRANG'S CITY OF REFUGE AT VOREE AND HIS KINGDOM ON AN ISLAND IN LAKE MICHIGAN.

Nestling between hills east of the city of La Crosse is the pleasant little valley known as Mormon coulée. Industrious Swiss and German farmers, who rigidly adhere to the severe orthodoxy of the Calvinistic creed, have reared on its wooded hillsides and beside the quiet little brook that meanders through, their comfortable cabins and farmhouses. Only the name of the coulée and a few crumbling ruins of masonry remain of what fifty years ago was a flourishing Mormon colony.[1]

Half a century ago a prosperous community of 2,000 persons inhabited the city of Voree, on the edge of a prairie skirted by White river, in the fertile county of Walworth. It was a stake of Zion, heralded to fugitive Mormons as a city of refuge. To-day the site of this city of promise is as bare as if its soil had never borne the weight of human habitation.[2]

[1] "Not many years ago the buildings erected by them were still standing, among which a lime-kiln which had been used by them was discovered."—"History of La Crosse County," p. 355.

[2] On the Old Geneva Road, in Walworth County, in the midst of a large corn field, is the only Mormon church in Wisconsin. The worshipers who congregate there belong to the Iowa Saints, known as "Young Josephites." They abhor both the Brighamite and Strangite doctrines. The church is situated at a cross-roads, almost within view of beautiful Geneva Lake, six or seven miles south of Elkhorn. Glancing to the four points of the compass, one sees great fields of waving corn, interspersed here and there with a strip of yellow barley glinting in the sunlight, or a clump of trees through which peers a substantial looking farmhouse. The little church is a plain building with belfry, neatly painted white, and bearing on a tablet above the wide front door this legend in raised letters of wood:

LATTER DAY SAINTS' CHURCH.

Much prejudice exists among the country people of the neighborhood against the forty or fifty Mormons who attend this church. Several years ago I spent a few days in the vicinity, for the purpose of gathering data relative to this community. I was told, with bated breath, several

On the largest island of the Beaver archipelago, in Lake Michigan, there flourished about the middle of the present century, a community of several thousand Latter-Day Saints. They were ruled by a king for nearly seven years. Of his temple and his so-called castle, the only vestiges now are a few splinters in the collections of relic hunters. His subjects have been scattered far and wide, and ax and torch long ago reduced their habitations to heaps of cinders.

In the busy brain of James Jesse Strang was conceived the scheme of founding in Wisconsin an empire of Latter-Day Saints. When the great exodus from Nauvoo began, he sought to turn the steps of the wanderers to his city of refuge at Voree. It was questionable for a time whether he or Brigham Young would triumph. Other pretenders sought to don the fallen mantle of Joseph Smith, but Brigham Young feared none of them as he did Strang. In the end the dream of Strang faded away, and his life paid the penalty of his ambition. His vast plans were "dead sea fruit, that tempt the eye, but turn to ashes on the lips."[a]

<h3 style="text-align:center">THE MORMON COULEE SETTLEMENT.</h3>

The settlement in Mormon coulée had but brief duration. When the Mormon temple at Nauvoo was planned, a party of Saints ascended the Mississippi to obtain lumber for the structure. Doubtless the snug little valleys behind the hills that skirt the prairie of La Crosse tempted them to there plant

instances of witchcraft attributable to the elder of the community. The narrators evidently believed the stories implicitly, the grotesqueness and impossibility of the performances alleged to have occurred scarcely paralleling in extent the credulity of the country folk.

In the neighboring village of Springfield there were, at the time of my visit, a few Mormons who used the schoolhouse as a meeting place. When the Saints were to be called together, the clangor of the school bell apprised them of the fact. Yielding to popular pressure, the trustees of the school had the bell removed. Thereupon the Mormons expressed their indignation by placarding the town with notices of their meeting, these words appearing in large, black type: "Curfew must not ring to-night."

[3] Scattered throughout the peninsula of Door County and adjacent islands, and also in the counties of Rock, Walworth and Racine, loyal adherents of King Strang can still be found. They cling to the faith he taught them with unabated devotion, and cherish his memory with unwavering loyalty.

an isolated stake of Zion.[4] At this time (1843) the prairie
was a mere trading station, and its rough inhabitants regarded
the Mormons as legitimate prey. There were frequent colli-
sions, due in part to the rude attentions bestowed upon the
Mormon women by the young men of the prairie. One night
the eastern heavens were all aglow. The Mormons had
secretly constructed rafts, removed their belongings to them
under cover of night, and applied the torch to their deserted
homes. Before the hostile inhabitants of the prairie could
intercept or molest them, their rafts had floated them many
miles away with the rapid current of the Mississippi.

The Mormon coulée settlement was governed by Elder
Lyman Wight, who later became an aspirant for the leadership
of the Church. Disappointed in his ambition, he led his adherents to Texas.[5]

KING STRANG'S STRANGE CAREER.

So closely is the story of Mormonism in Wisconsin and
Michigan associated with James Strang, that its recital is largely
biographical. Of his boyhood little is known, except that he
was studious and ambitious—and likewise eccentric. After
his death there was found among his papers the fragments of an
autobiography covering the period of his life up to the age
of 12. The writing comes to a sudden stop, as if the writer had
been disturbed and had never cared, or perhaps had no opportunity, to resume the story of his life. In view of the later

[4] While en route for the copper mines of Lake Superior, Alfred Brun-
son of Prairie du Chien and his party of prospectors came to the Black
River in May, 1842. "We found the Mormons in possession getting out
timber for their Nauvoo temple; to them and to our company I preached
the first gospel sermon ever delivered in that valley. We ferried over
Black River on their keel boats, except the cattle, who swam."—"History
of the Chippewa Valley," by Thos. E. Randall, p. 23.
   George Z. Heuston, of Winona, informs me, on the authority of his
father's manuscript history of Trempealeau County, that about that same
time a few Mormon families settled in the vicinity of the modern town of
Trempealeau, at a place called Little Tamarack, but they did not remain
long, and probably joined Lyman Wight's colony at La Crosse.

[5] An excellent condensed sketch of Lyman Wight, with extracts
from his journal, appears on page 125 of "The Wights, a Record of Thomas
Wight of Dedham and Medfield and of His Descendants, 1635-1896."

career of this strange man, the fragment is interesting as giving
an insight into the unusual elements that tinctured his life and
fashioned his character.[6]

"My infancy was a period of continual sickness and extreme
suffering," he wrote, "and I have understood that at one time I
was so low as to be thought dead, and that preparations were
made for my burial. All my early recollections are painful,
and at this day I am utterly unable to comprehend the feeling
of those who look back with pleasure on their infancy, and
regret the rapid passing away of childhood. Till I had children
of my own, happy in their infantile gambols, the recollection of
those days produced a creeping sensation akin to terror."

It was the claim of Strang that he was a descendant of
Henry de l'Estrange, who accompanied the Duke of York on
his expedition for the conquest of New Amsterdam. In his
autobiography he notes that his father, Clement Strang, was
the fifth son of Gabriel Strang. Coming originally of a
Norman stock, "they have continually intermarried with the
Dutch and German families of the Hudson, and therefore par-
take more of the German type than any other. Counting continually in the male line for ten generations back, our ancestors
are Jews, but so large is the admixture of other blood that the
Semitic type seems to be quite lost."[7]

On his mother's side, Strang's ancestry was of the purest
Yankee stock from Rhode Island. His mother's maiden name
was James.

On a farm in the town of Scipio, N. Y., owned by his father,
James Jesse Strang was born March 21, 1813. He was but 3
years of age when his parents removed to Hanover, in Cha-
tauqua county, his life until manhood being passed there. The
meager facilities of a country school were supplemented by a

---

[6] I am indebted to Chas. J. Strang, of Lansing, Mich., son of King
Strang, for a copy of the manuscript.

[7] See autobiography, appendix.

brief term at Fredonia Academy. Such details of his life at this period as are known indicate that he was an omniverous reader, and that he was noted for a remarkably retentive memory. In the local debating clubs he vanquished all opponents. While working on a farm he borrowed law books and eagerly read and digested them. He was admitted to the bar and began to practice in Mayville, later removing to Ellington. He became postmaster there, but he was of too restless a spirit to remain long in one place. Although married shortly after he was admitted to the bar, he began a roving life, going from one place to another and flitting from one occupation to another without particular motive, except to follow the bent of his nature. He taught a country school, edited a newspaper at Randolph, and then took the rostrum as a temperance lecturer. He was full of energy and ambition, and a remarkably ready and effective speaker.

Strang's wife was Mary Perce. Her brother resided at Burlington, in Racine county, Wis., and it was at his solicitation that the young man removed to this state. This was in 1843. Here he resumed the practice of law, forming a partnership with C. P. Barnes, who later became associated as a practitioner with Judge Wm. P. Lyon.[8]

In the year following his removal to Wisconsin, there came to Burlington several itinerant missionaries from the Mormon Church at Nauvoo, seeking proselytes. Their talk appealed with peculiar fascination to the temperament of Strang. He threw himself heart and soul into the movement. It was a field that afforded his peculiar talents full play. Before six months had expired, Strang had developed from an humble convert to

---

[8] Following incident, told the writer by Judge Lyon, illustrates the peculiar bent of Strang's mind: "On one accasion he brought a suit before me (I was then a justice of the peace) to recover the value of honey which he claimed had been stolen from his client's apiary by the thievish bees of a neighbor. Who ever heard of a law suit based on such grounds? And yet Strang conducted the case with great shrewdness and made a most plausible argument. He was continually bringing up unexpected points in law cases, and using arguments that would have been thought of by no one else. I think he liked the notoriety that resulted from that sort of thing."

the self-styled head of the Church. It was in January, 1844, that his zeal was kindled. He visited Nauvoo, and on the 25th of February was baptized by the seer Joseph Smith into the communion of Latter-Day Saints. The prophet conceived a great regard for the young zealot from Wisconsin, and but a week after baptism Strang had been made an elder with authority to plant a stake of Zion in the immediate neighborhood of his Wisconsin home.

With restless energy and marvelous success, Strang began his propaganda and laid the foundation for the city of Voree. What his ideas were can only be conjectured in the light of his subsequent dream of empire. Intensely ambitious for power, versed in the arts that enable leadership of men, fired with religious fervor, keenly conscious of his own abilities, the example of Joseph Smith's success doubtless inspired him with great ambitions.[9] He saw in Smith an uneducated man who from the humblest origin became in the course of but a few years the unchallenged prophet of many thousands of men and women.[10] The possibilities of his own future dazzled him. Events at first conspired to bring to immediate realization the dreams of Strang. In June the prophet and his brother Hyrum were riddled with bullets by a mob at Carthage, in the state of . Illinois. On whom should the mantle fall that the martyred seer had worn? Many sought the succession; but one of them possessed the energy or capacity to measure weapons for more than a brief period with the masterful craft of Brigham Young. That one was Strang.[11] That Young feared Strang most

[9] "E. D. Howe, in his valuable work, Mormonism Unveiled (Painesville, O., 1834), presents the testimonials of eighty-one persons, neighbors and acquaintances of the Smith family, all attesting to their illiteracy and generally worthless and disreputable character."—"The Prophet of Palmyra," p. 11.

[10] "Joseph estimated that, in the various quarters of the earth where his religion had been preached, he had over a hundred and fifty thousand followers."—Remy & Brenchley's "Journey to Great Salt Lake City," Vol. I, p. 349.

[11] "Of all the aspirants he (Strang) was the only one, save Brigham Young, who displayed any genuine qualities of leadership."—Michigan Pioneer and Historical Collections, Vol. XVIII, p. 5.

is attested by the bitterness with which in pamphlets and in Mormon newspapers Strang was assailed, while the other pretenders were almost ignored as if unworthy of notice.

In the struggle that ensued between Brigham Young and James Jesse Strang, the former had all the advantage of an entrenched position. He was one of the all-powerful Council of Twelve, and at first fed the enmity of his colleagues towards outside aspirants by ingenuously suggesting to each individually hopes of personal aggrandizement.[12]   It was a shrewd scheme to first crush outside aspirants, and then narrow down rivalry at home by cajolery or intimidation till his own elevation became possible.

Despite the hostility of the combined Council of Twelve,[13] Strang made a vigorous and resourceful campaign to secure the prophetic succession.   Joseph Smith's Nauvoo followers had not recovered from the shock of their leader's assassination before Strang was in their midst exhorting them to follow him to the city of promise in Wisconsin.   He exhibited a letter purporting to have been written by the seer just before his assassination, prophesying that he would soon wear "the double crown of martyr and king in a heavenly world," and appointing James Strang as his successor:

"And now behold my servant, James J. Strang, hath come to thee from far for truth when he knew it not, and hath not

---

[12] The twelve apostles, after the death of the prophet, bestowed these names upon each other:
Brigham Young, the Lion of the Lord.
Heber C. Kimball, the Herald of Grace.
Parley P. Pratt, the Archer of Paradise.
Orson Hyde, the Olive Branch of Israel.
Willard Richards, the Keeper of the Rolls.
John Taylor, the Champion of Right.
William Smith, the Patriarchal Staff of Jacob.
William Woodruff, the Banner of the Gospel.
George A. Smith, the Entablature of Truth.
Orson Pratt, the Gauge of Philosophy.
John E. Page, the Sundial.
Lyman Wight, the Wild Ram of the Mountains.

[13] Two of them—George A. Smith and John E. Page—subsequently enrolled themselves under the standard of Strang. Their names frequently appear in the conference reports published in the Voree Herald and Northern Islander.

rejected it, but had faith in thee, the Shepherd and Stone of Israel, and to him shall the gathering of the people be, for he shall plant a stake of Zion in Wisconsin, and I will establish it; and there shall my people have peace and rest and shall not be moved, for it shall be established on the prairie on White river, in the lands of Racine and Walworth; and behold my servants James and Aaron shall plant it, for I have given them wisdom, and Daniel shall stand in his lot on the hill beside the river looking down on the prairie, and shall instruct my people and shall plead with them face to face.

"Behold my servant James shall lengthen the cords and strengthen the stakes of Zion, and my servant Aaron shall be his counselor, for he hath wisdom in the gospel and understandeth the doctrines and erreth not therein.

"And I will have a house built unto me there of stone, and there will I show myself to my people by many mighty works, and the name of the city shall be called Voree, which is, being interpreted, garden of peace; for there shall my people have peace and rest and wax fat and pleasant in the presence of their enemies.

"But I will again stretch out my arm over the river of waters, and on the banks thereof shall the house of my choice be. But now the city of Voree shall be a stronghold of safety to my people, and they that are faithful and obey me, I will there give them great prosperity, and such as they have not had before; and unto Voree shall be the gathering of my people, and there shall the oppressed flee for safety and none shall hurt or molest them."[14]

The Council of Twelve made a furious onslaught on the pretensions of Strang; denounced his letter as a forgery, and threatened with the thunders of the Church all who would

---

[14] Letter of Joseph Smith to James J. Strang, published in "The Diamond," p. 3.

uphold the pretender.[15] The Brighamites started the story that the postmark on the letter was black, whereas all Nauvoo letters were stamped in red. Strang produced the letter and showed a red postmark. He claimed that the letter was received at Burlington by regular course of mail, through the Chicago distributing office; that it bore the Nauvoo postmark of June 19, the day following its date, and that C. P. Barnes, a well-known Burlington lawyer, took the letter out of the post-office and delivered it to Strang July 9. It was also claimed by the Brighamites that no proper entry of the mailing of such a letter could be found in the register of "mails sent" from Nauvoo. When it was sought to verify Strang's claim that the proper entry was there, the register had mysteriously disappeared.

With much shrewdness, the Council of Twelve spread abroad among the people the doctrine that the martyred prophet could have no successor, and their united opposition disposed of the pretensions of several claimants, among them Sidney Rigdon, Lyman Wight and William Smith. The most vigorous claimant was Strang. Fortified with the letter alleged to have been sent him by Joseph Smith, and loudly proclaiming its genuineness among the Nauvooites, he soon gathered a considerable following. The twelve apostles summoned a conference. With much force and logic Strang defended his position, citing liberally from the Bible, the Book of Mormon and the Book of Doctrines and Covenants. The apostles contended that no man could assume the prophetic succession and hold the keys of authority which Joseph had obtained from the hands of angels. Their official organs, published at Nauvoo and Liverpool, had before this proclaimed in no uncertain words the doctrine that to take Joseph's place as seer, revelator and prophet was mere usurpation.

---

[15] The columns of the "Times and Seasons," published at Nauvoo, fairly teem with denunciation of the pretender, Strang.

"Let no man presume for a moment his place will be filled by another," were the words reiterated in the "Times and Seasons" and in the "Millennial Star," whose columns were controlled by the twelve and their abettors.   In the face of the sentiment thus created, Strang made a hopeless appeal for recognition.   His pretensions were rejected, and with the usual formulas of the Church ritual, he was "given over to the buffetings of Satan."

THE CITY OF REFUGE.

Strang was not so easily disposed of, however.   With a body of recusant Mormons whom his remarkable powers of oratory had attached to his cause, he returned to Voree and began to build up his city of refuge, prophesying that the Mormons would be driven from Nauvoo by the Lamanites,[16] and that then the words of Joseph would be realized.   In every detail he carried out the policy by which the seer Joseph had appealed to his followers.   He pretended to have revelations. These he transcribed in imitation of scriptural language, teeming with vague phrases upon which he placed such interpretations as were needful to carry out his immediate purposes.   He organized his church on the pattern prescribed by the sacred books of the Mormon faith, with a council of twelve, and quorums of elders and priests.   Over all of them he exercised supreme authority.   Like Joseph, when schism threatened or murmurs of discontent came to his ears, he would silence all opposition by means of a convenient revelation.[17]

[16] According to the "Book of Mormon," a remnant of the tribe of Joseph was miraculousy led to the new world across the Pacific Ocean (Book of Nephi), and separated into two distinct nations—Nephites and Lamanites.

"This division was caused by a certain portion of them being greatly persecuted, because of their righteousness, by the remainder. The persecuted nation migrated toward the northern parts of North America, leaving the wicked nation in possession of the middle and southern parts of the same. The former were called Nephites, being led by a prophet who was called Nephi. The latter were called Lamanites, being led by a very wicked man whose name was Laman."—Kidder's "Mormonism and the Mormons." p. 267.

[17] "Revelations of James J. Strang," collected and printed in pamphlet form by Wingfield Watson after the death of Strang—now an excessively rare pamphlet.

The crowning achievement, and one which disturbed the authorities at Nauvoo considerably, was the finding of buried plates near the city of Voree. These he called the Plates of Laban. The cabalistic hieroglyphics which he transcribed by means of the Urim and Thummim,[18] were claimed by him to be the long-lost Book of the Law of the Lord, admirably supplementing the Book of Mormon which Joseph Smith had in like manner translated from the plates dug out of the hill of Cumorah, in the state of New York.

None of these artifices were original with Strang. Joseph Smith had employed them all. But there was shrewd method, rather than lack of originality, in this imitation. Doubtless Strang's purpose was to verify his pretension that the prophetic succession had devolved upon himself. In no manner could he have appealed more forcibly to the religious delusion entertained by the followers of Joseph Smith.

The twelve apostles whom he sent as missionaries to New York, Philadelphia, Baltimore and elsewhere in the east encountered in bitter controversy the proselyting agents of Brigham Young. His press at Voree turned out thousands of pamphlets aiming to show the hollow spuriousness of the doctrines enunciated by Brigham Young's followers. The Voree Herald contained as bitter tirades against them as did the Nauvoo Times and Seasons against himself. He displayed tremendous energy with tongue and pen, and the reports of conferences in the Voree Herald give evidence of it. The Liverpool paper published by the Mormons also assailed

---

[18] The Urim and Thummim consisted, according to the statement of Lucy Smith, mother of the prophet, of two transparent stones, clear as crystals, set in the two rims of a bow.

"Urim and Thummim (Lights and Perfections). These were the sacred symbols (worn upon the breastplate of the high priest, 'upon his heart'), by which God gave oracular responses for the guidance of his people in temporal matters. What they were is unknown. Some scholars suppose that they were the twelve stones of the breastplate; others that they were two additional stones concealed in its fold. Josephus adds to these the two sardonyx buttons worn on the shoulders, which, he says, emitted luminous rays when the response was favorable; but the precise mode in which the oracles were given is lost in obscurity."—"Glossary of Antiquities" in Oxford edition of the Bible, p. 150.

Strang with great bitterness. These are the headlines of an
article nearly four columns in length:

SKETCHES OF NOTORIOUS CHARACTERS.

James J. Strang, Successor of Sidney Rigdon, Judas
Iscariot, Cain & Co., Envoy Extraordinary
and Minister Plenipotentiary of His
Most Gracious Majesty, Lucifer
the I., etc. [19]

In Philadelphia, Aug. 30, 1846, Strang found Orson Hyde
and J. Taylor, two of his old-time opponents, holding meetings.
He challenged them to a public debate to show who had the
best authority to represent the true Mormon faith. This was
the answer he received:[20]

SIR—After Lucifer was cut off and thrust down to hell, we have no
knowledge that God ever condescended to investigate the subject or right
of authority with him.
Your case has been disposed of by the authorities of the church, and
being satisfied with our own power and calling, we have no disposition to
ask from whence yours came.

Yours respectfully.
ORSON HYDE.
JOHN TAYLOR.

It must be admitted that in the numerous pamphlets which
he scattered broadcast, and in his newspaper rejoinders, Strang
kept his temper much better than the Nauvoo disputants. In
his pamphlet called "Prophetic Controversy," he sarcastically
alludes to the "saintly spirit" that could inspire such fulmina-
tions as have been quoted; but his failure to secure recognition
at Nauvoo rankled deeply. In his Gospel Tract No. 4, wherein
he defends "the calling of James J. Strang as successor to
Joseph Smith," this serious charge is made:[21]

"Immediately after the martyrdom of Joseph, John Taylor,
Willard Richards and William W. Phelps took a kind of tem-
porary direction of the affairs of the Church, instructing the
saints to wait patiently the hand of the Lord, assuring them that
He had not left them without a shepherd, and that all things

[19] "Millennial Star," Vol. VIII, p. 123.
[20] "Gospel Herald," Vol. I, No. 8.
[21] "Gospel Tract No. 4," Voree, Wis., 1848, p. 5.

would be made known in due season.   To every question of the saints, who is the prophet, replies were made in substance that the saints would know in due season, but that nothing could be done till the Twelve got home, because the appointment of a prophet and the directions for salvation of the Church from the perils they were in was contained in sealed packages directed to them.   Orson Hyde and others of the Twelve who were then in the east, stated in public congregations in New York, Philadelphia and other cities that Willard Richards had written to them that the appointment of a prophet was left with him under seal to be opened on the return of the Twelve.   This assertion was so often made that the whole Church was daily expecting to hear a new prophet proclaimed.   On the 8th of August, 1844, when Sidney Rigdon endeavored to obtain authority to lead the Church, John P. Green, marshal of the city of Nauvoo, told them 'they need not trouble themselves about it, for Joseph had appointed one James J. Strang, who lived up north, to stand in his stead.'   The sudden death of John P. Green, immediately after this declaration (under very extraordinary circumstances), left Willard Richards and John Taylor sole repositors of all documents on this subject, except this letter. They had simply to suppress documents in their hands to set themselves up in power, or overthrow themselves and their pretensions by publishing them."

THE GREAT EXODUS.

The great exodus of Mormons across the Mississippi and into the wilderness of the west began early in February, 1846. Long before this, however, the knot had been tightening around the doomed city of Nauvoo.   Every man's hand was uplifted against the Mormons, and conflicts frequently occurred between the Saints and their neighbors outside the fold. Strang's prolific press at Voree turned out thousands of copies of what he termed "the first pastoral letter of James, the

Prophet." It bore date of December 25, 1845, and concluded in this wise:

"Let not my call to you be vain. The destroyer has gone forth among you, and has prevailed. You are preparing to resign country and houses and lands to him. Many of you are about to leave the haunts of civilization and of men to go into an unexplored wilderness among savages, and in trackless deserts, to seek a home in the wilds where the footprint of the

STRANG'S "CASTLE" ON BEAVER ISLAND.
(From a photograph owned by Chas. J. Strang.)

white man is not found. The voice of God has not called you to this. His promise has not gone before to prepare a habitation for you. The hearts of the Lamanites are not turned unto you, and they will not regard you. When the herd comes, the savages shall pursue. The cloud which surrounds by day shall bewilder, and the pillar of fire by night shall consume and reveal you to the destroyer.

"Let the oppressed flee for safety unto Voree, and let the gathering of the people be there. * * * Let the filth of Zion be cleansed, and her garments of peace put on. Let neither gun nor sword be lifted in defiance, nor rest be taken upon arm of flesh, and the city of our God shall be saved, and the temple of His holiness be unpolluted by the hand of the Gentile."

By the exodus of the Brighamites across the Mississippi, Strang's colony at Voree alone remained in the northwest of the thousands who had embraced the faith of Joseph Smith. Sidney Rigdon had led a small contingent into Pennsylvania; Lyman Wight a few followers to Texas; Smith a little remnant to a corner of Illinois; these were offshoots that came to naught. At Voree the numbers constantly increased. Missionaries were sent to the east to seek converts; the press turned out pamphlets to be scattered broadcast. Regularly the Voree Herald was issued for distribution among the faithful. Some internal dissensions arose from time to time, but Strang easily disposed of them. The minutes of one of the conferences note that Lorenzo Dow Hickey was suspended by the prophet James for "most gross lying and slander upon Brother G. J. Adams and Samuel Graham, and neglecting his mission to follow after the diabolical revelations of Increase McGee Van Dusen." At another conference the apostasy of John E. Page, president of the Twelve, was the subject of comment, and this resolution was spread upon the minutes:

"*Resolved*, That we deliver him over to the buffetings of Satan until he repent."

In spite of occasional backslidings, the city of Voree grew and flourished. The Saints at first "met in a grove," as the conference minutes state, but a splendid temple was planned. In a letter descriptive of the edifice, Geo. J. Adams wrote Aug. 27, 1849:

"The temple is going up steadily and constantly, and a most beautiful structure it will be when finished. It covers two and one-sixth acres of ground, has twelve towers, and the great hall 200 feet square in the center. The entire walls are eight feet through, the floors and roofs are to be marble, and when finished it will be the grandest building in the world. The strong Tower of Zion is being erected on the Hill of Promise, the walls of which are three or four feet thick, which when finished is for the carrying out of the order of Enoch in all its beauty and fulness."[22]

STRANG'S KINGDOM OF ST. JAMES.

It soon became apparent to Strang that the same conditions which had driven the Mormons of Nauvoo to a trans-Mississippi wilderness, would endanger the permanency of his colony in the course of a few years. For the growth of a Mormon community isolation was essential; where Gentile influences controlled the vicinage, there the utter annihilation of Mormonism was but a question of time. In his wanderings he had caught a glimpse from a vessel's deck of the natural beauty and seeming fruitfulness of a cluster of islands near the door that divides the great inland seas of Huron and Michigan. Here was an ideal seat of power, remote from the obtrusiveness of civil officers whose view of laws might differ from his own; yet not so distant from the line of travel as to render profitable traffic impossible. The waters teemed with excellent fish; the forests would furnish an abundance of most excellent timber; the soil needed but to be scratched to yield in multiplied plenty. To this land of promise could he lead his Saints, and here would they wax fat and strong.

If this was Strang's dream of empire, as subsequent events indicated, the beginnings were indeed humble. He is authority for the statement that he fixed on the islands in Lake Michi-

---

[22] "Voree Herald," August, 1849.

gan as a place for a Mormon community in 1846.[23]   Nearly a
year elapsed before his plans could be set in motion.   With
four companions he took passage on a little hooker, the captain
agreeing to land them on Beaver Island.   They sold their
blankets to pay their passage, and on the 11th day of May
stepped from the little sailing vessel upon the soil of the land
which the leader prophetically declared would prove to them
an inheritance.   They were without a cent of money, but had
provisions enough to last two days.   Their reception was
inhospitable in the extreme.   At neither of the two trading
houses then on the island could five penniless men arrange for
lodging, so they sought the shelter of the woods.   Construct-
ing a camp of hemlock boughs, they undertook a thorough
exploration of the island.   Leeks and beechnuts served for
food while they were thus engaged.

Their perseverance brought its reward.   They soon
obtained employment, and it was not long before they had
accumulated a store of provisions, built a log cabin and
arranged for the use of a boat.   Strang and two of the men
returned to Voree to start the migration to the new land of
promise.   Winter locked upon the island a Mormon population of five men and thirteen women and children.   The following winter the Mormons on the island numbered sixty-two,
seventeen of them being men.   In the summer of 1849 saints
began to arrive in considerable numbers.   Instead of confin-
ing their efforts to working for the traders at the harbor, they
now felt numerically strong enough to begin for themselves.
Twelve elders went in various directions to summon the faithful
to the new stake of Zion, and to seek additional converts.   The
islanders began the construction of a schooner, built a steam
saw mill and made a road to the interior, where the land was
excellently adapted for agriculture.   They manifested so much
energy that the fishermen whose rude huts punctuated the

---

[23]   "Ancient and Modern Michillmackinac," 1854, p. 22.

coast here, as well as on the mainland opposite, took serious alarm.   A land sale being held about this time, considerable friction occurred between Mormon and Gentile claimants of choice tracts.   There arose an unpleasantness that later bore bitter fruit.   It was claimed by the Saints that the fishermen induced the captains of vessels bearing Mormon emigrants not to land at the Beaver.   Many were carried on to Wisconsin who had been ticketed from the east for the harbor of St. James, for so the Mormons had rechristened the horseshoe bend where vessels came to land, and where in stormy weather they found a safe haven.

It was not long before the Mormons bade fair to control the island.   They but believed that they had come into their own, for this was the revelation given unto their seer and revelator long before their coming: "So I beheld a land amidst wide waters and covered with large timber, with a deep broad bay on one side of it; and I wandered over it upon little hills and among rich valleys, where the air was pure and serene, and the unfolding foliage, with its fragrant shades, attracted me till I wandered to bright clear waters scarcely ruffled by the breeze. * * * And one came near unto me, and I said, What meaneth this?   And he answered and said, Behold, here shall God establish His people.   * * *   For He will make their arm strong, and their bow shall abide in strength, and they shall not bow to the oppressor, and the power of the Gentile shall not be upon them, for the arm of God shall be with them to support.   * * *   It hath abundance in the riches of the forest, and in the riches of the earth, and in the riches of the waters.   And the Lord God shall add possession unto the faithful, and give good gifts unto them that keep His law, and He will establish them therein forever."[24]

To appreciate the spirit animating the Saints in thus taking possession, one must realize the fervor of their faith in the reve-

[24] "Revelations of James J. Strang." p. 5.

lation of their seer. There were among them some who had in mind mere pelf and plunder, but the greater number of the misled people was no doubt inspired by fanatic zeal. The law of Moses was their law, supplemented by the doctrines of Mormon and the visions of Strang. To follow these injunctions was to do no wrong, no matter what laws of the land they violated. Like the children of Israel, they were going from the wilderness to a land overflowing with milk and honey. As the people led by Moses had ruthlessly slain the Amorites, the Amalakites and the Midianites, so they felt justified in smiting the Lamanites, or Gentiles. There was this distinction, that they lived in an age when prudence forbade violent physical onslaught upon neighboring inhabitants, and legal strategy took the place of physical violence. This, at least, was the policy of the leaders, and they were implicitly obeyed as a rule.

The Mormons manifested their sense of ownership by giving new names to the physical distinctions of Beaver Island. The beautiful land-locked harbor was called St. James. The cluster of houses that were reared on the ancient mounds along the shore—in the eyes of the Mormons the evidences of an extinct race alluded to in the Book of Mormon—they dignified by the name City of St. James. A hill in the interior received the biblical name of Mount Pisgah. The river Jordan discharged into the lake the waters that poured into its bed from the Sea of Galilee. Thus did the nomenclature of the island receive the distinctive impress of its Mormon population.

Encounters between Mormons and Gentiles soon became frequent. The Mormons planned a large tabernacle. While some of them were getting out the timber for the structure, they were set upon and soundly beaten. Doubtless there is much truth in the claim made by the Mormons that up to this time they were more sinned against than aggressors. Drunken fishermen invaded their homes and subjected the women to indignities; debating clubs were attended by uninvited guests, whose boisterous conduct prevented proceedings. Men from old Michilimackinac came in boats to raid outlying farm-houses. Families sent by the missionary elders were met at the wharf and told to return to the boat, as all the Mormons would soon be driven away or killed.   ·

About the year 1850 the Saints began to retaliate in earnest. Their numbers had so increased that they could safely do so. The ambitions of Strang were about being realized. He had reorganized his community of Saints. The Book of the Law of the Lord, which he had "translated" from plates dug out of the hill at Voree, had added another sacred book to the Mormon library, ranking in the faith of the Beaver Islanders with the Bible and the Book of Mormon. "Written on metallic plates long previous to the Babylonish captivity," as Strang explained to his credulous followers, the Urim and Thummim brought to him by an angel's hand had enabled him to interpret the characters thereof. Thus had he restored to the chosen people the ancient manuscript long lost to the Jewish nation. The sacred book kept in the ark of the covenant and lost when the children of Israel were hurried into captivity, came back after all these centuries by revelation given to Strang.[25]

And the Beaver Island Mormons believed what he said.

"The Calling of a King" was the caption of Chapter XX of the Book of the Law of the Lord, and therein appeared these words as the sixth section:

"6. He (God) hath chosen His servant James to be King: He hath made him His Apostle to all nations: He hath established Him a Prophet above the Kings of the earth; and appointed him King in Zion: By His voice did He call him, and He sent His angels unto him to ordain him."

WAR WITH THE FISHERMEN.

The 8th of July, 1850, was set for the coronation of King Strang, and great preparations were made for the event. In

---

[25] "Book of the Law of the Lord," preface.

the meantime a plot had been hatched which threatened the extinction of the budding kingdom. But for the energetic measures taken by Strang, doubtless there would have been a bloody conflict between the fishermen and the Mormons. This is Strang's account of the affair:

"In May, 1850, a general invitation was given on all the fishing grounds to come to Whiskey Point against the 4th of July, for a glorious and patriotic celebration of Independence— to be consummated by the expulsion of the Mormons. In this invitation all the traders at Beaver, as well as the fishermen, joined. Material aid was furnished from Mackinac, and several small vessels owned there engaged to go to Beaver with supplies, and lay in the harbor ready to join in the fray. Arms, ammunition and provisions (of which whiskey was chief article) were laid in; and the Gentiles expressed the utmost confidence of success.

"On their part the Mormons gave notice of a general assembly, and by that means called in a great number of their brethren from distant places, some of whom brought arms. A cannon and a stock of powder and lead was purchased; a regular guard enrolled, who were on duty nightly, while others were drilling. This was conducted with the utmost secrecy, all affecting to believe that no attack would be made. They also procured a large schooner from Chicago for the occasion, which they anchored in the harbor, and in the night filled with armed men, who kept below the deck.

"On the 3d of July several boats arrived at Whiskey Point from the fishing grounds, filled with armed men. One vessel from Mackinac arrived and anchored in the harbor. During the night they had a carouse, in the course of which Mr. Strang, with a select party, reconnoitred their quarters, ascertained their plans, numbers, etc., poured some of their powder in the lake, and put tobacco in one of their barrels of whiskey, by means of which those who drank of it became excessively drunk.

"The plan was to go to the meeting singly and in small groups, with slung shot and other concealed weapons; but affecting order and propriety, and get seats nearly as possible in a body, in the region of the speakers' stand and clerks' tables. In the progress of the service they were to commence talking, drinking, swearing, etc., and if anyone interfered or attempted to keep order, begin a fight; and falling suddenly on the unprepared congregation with pistols, bowie knives and slung shot, disperse them and disable or kill all the leaders before they had time to rally, arm or make a stand. This was to be followed up by a general debauchery of the women and burning of houses.

"At the first dawn of the Fourth, the Mormons commenced firing a national salute, which was the first intimation to the Gentiles that they had a cannon. They were not a little alarmed when they discovered that at every boom of the cannon the balls skipped along the water past Whiskey Point, scarcely two rods from them, and were regularly getting the range for their buildings. Before their surprise had time to abate, McKinley, who was proprietor there, was waited on by a deputation of Mormons with the notice that as he had made his place the headquarters of the mob, he would be held responsible for any attack from any quarter; and the first gun fired would be the signal for destroying his establishment and every soul in it. Notice was also given to all the Gentiles having property on the island, that if they joined in, furnished or even associated with the mob, they would be taken as enemies and their homes made as bare as a sand bank.

"The Mormons met within the unfinished walls of the tabernacle; eight men mounted guard, with their guns shotted; the cannon unlimbered in front, in charge of twelve artillerists, with a fire in which heated balls were continually ready; and two patrols and a water guard were constantly on the lookout for the enemy.

"In the course of the day two vessels and sixteen boats arrived from the fisheries, bringing men, munition, etc., including one cannon; but no hostile movements were made till afternoon, when a company of Gentile women came into the congregation unattended. Directly one of them left and returned to the boat which had carried her over, and had a conversation with nine men who were with it. They went up and were allowed to enter the congregation, but as soon as they were seated it was announced from the stand that any interruption of the service or business would be instantly punished by personal chastisement; and the guard were charged in case any general disorder was attempted, to cut down every person who joined in it. They sat uneasily a few moments and asked leave to withdraw. The guard conducted them out and compelled them to take their boat and leave.

"The following evening during their carouse at Whiskey Point, a select party of the Mormons contrived to get within hearing of them at their consultation, and learned that they had been disappointed by the non-arrival of the Gull Island, Seuil Choix and East shore fishermen; that part of the resident traders were anxious to postpone the attempt, in the fear that it would be a failure and the Mormons would take revenge on them for their part in the transaction; that jealousies existed among them as to the means by which the Mormons had obtained their plans; and the sober were fearful that the Mormons were too well prepared. Indecision and disorder prevailed, and they were unable to agree upon their leader. The result of all these embarrassments was that they generally agreed to 'wait for recruits and then pay off the damned Mormons for arming and setting guards before anybody meddled with them.' "[26]

---

[26] "Ancient and Modern Michillmackinac," p. 25.

CORONATION OF KING JAMES.

The threatened invasion having miscarried, the coronation of the King proceeded according to program. On the 8th of July, 1850, a date that became known as "King's Day," Strang assumed royal powers. This is an account of the ceremony in the words of an eye-witness, Mrs. Cecelia Hill, now of Wonewoc, Wis., then a young woman living with her Mormon parents on Beaver Island:[27]

"I was present when Strang was crowned King. The ceremony took place in the tabernacle, a building about 80 feet long, constructed of hewn logs, and but partly completed at the time of the coronation. Like any young woman under similar circumstances, I was anxious to be present and managed to get into the tabernacle. At one end was a platform, and towards it marched the procession of elders and other quorums, escorting the King. First came the King, dressed in a robe of bright red, and accompanied by his council. Then followed the twelve elders, the seventy and the minor orders of the ministry, or quorums, as they were called. The people were permitted to occupy what space remained in the tabernacle.

"The chief ceremonials were performed by George J. Adams, president of the council of elders. Adams was a man of imposing presence. He was over six feet tall, and he towered over the short-statured King. who, however, made up in intellect what he lacked in frame. Adams had been an actor, and he succeeded in making the crowning of the King a very imposing ceremony. It ended by placing upon the auburn head of King Strang a crown of metal. The crown was a plain circlet, with a cluster of stars projecting in front. It was July 8th, that this ceremony occurred, and every recurring 8th of July was known as the King's day and was celebrated as a holiday with many festivities. The entire population of the island would gather at a place in the woods to go through pre-

---

[27] See appendix, narrative of Mrs. Cecelia Hill.

scribed ceremonials—the hewers of wood and the drawers of water to make proper obeisance to the King. There were burnt offerings to begin with. The head of each family brought a fowl, and a heifer was thereupon killed. Its body was dissected without breaking a bone. After these ceremonials there was feasting and rejoicing, and the people danced on the greensward. King's day was the same with the islanders as the Fourth of July is with us."

King Strang was now supreme on Beaver Island, and bade fair to soon control the entire group of islands. His policy was to foster the fisheries as a source of profit to his colony, and to use the power of political machinery to secure immunity for infractions of the law. As the population of the island multiplied and the power of the Mormons with it, the hatred of the traders and fishermen on the opposite coasts became more intense. The border feud grew so bitter that the newspapers of Detroit, Cleveland, Buffalo and New York[28] devoted considerable space to its incidents. As a rule, these accounts represented the Mormons as a band of pirates engaged in plunder and crimes of all kinds. The center of the hostile camp was at old Mackinac, and here plans were made for discomfiting the Mormons. It is difficult at this day to judge how far the Gentiles were in the wrong and in how far the Mormons. Doubtless there was much wrong on both sides. "Such expressions as 'the earth is the Lord's and the fulness thereof,' and 'we are the Lord's chosen people' stilled the consciences and justified the use of property owned by others; yet it is undoubtedly true that many depredations were committed by irresponsible persons and deliberately charged to the Mormons."[29]

[28] "Rough Notes," a paper published at Buffalo, and the "Detroit Free Press" were particularly conspicuous in publishing reports of Mormon depredations. Strang published an elaborate defense in the "New York Tribune" of July 2, 1853.

[29] "Beaver Island and its Mormon Kingdom," by Chas. J. Strang, in "The Ottawan," p. 66.

At first the advantage was with the Gentiles at Mackinac, for they had the machinery of government in their hands. The sheriff aided them by arresting Mormons and taking them to Mackinac for trial. On one occasion Strang and a company of workmen had gone to Hog Island to save from the wreck of a vessel a yawl boat frozen in the shoals. A man named Moore, who had been chased off Beaver Island for selling whiskey, went before a justice of the peace at Mackinac and swore out a warrant for the arrest of thirty-one men on the novel charge that they had "put him in fear of danger." Sheriff Granger, with a posse of thirteen white men and thirty-two Indians, went to the island where the men were, seized the boat of the Mormons, and, believing their prey secure, proceeded to the camp of the Mormons a little past midnight. A wild Irish hurrah and an accompanying Indian war whoop awoke the Mormons to a night of terror and suffering. Hatless and shoeless they rushed into the woods and sought the protection of a swamp, while the sheriff's men plundered the camp and divided the spoils of war. The Mormons found a leaky fish boat at the opposite end of the island, and this they launched.. It was a cold April morning. According to the account they afterwards gave, "the lake was spotted with vast fields of drift ice. With a boat preserved from sinking only by the ice frozen in it, without sails or oar locks, and with three unsuitable oars; not half clothed, no provisions, without a line to tie their boat nor an ax to repair any accident, they set out on the broad blue waters for a place of safety."

It took twenty-four hours for them to reach Gull Island, and here they spent five miserable days in a fish shanty before they managed to repair the boat sufficiently to proceed. After this a price was set on Strang's head, and several hundred armed men, including Irish fishermen and Indians, hunted for him for weeks to earn the reward of $300 offered by the sheriff for the body of Strang, "dead or alive."[30]

---

[30] In a letter to the writer from Chas. J. Strang.

GOSPEL HERALD.

VOL. IV. No. 10.]   VOREE, Wis., THURSDAY, MAY 24, 1849.   [WHOLE No. 124.

GOSPEL HERALD,

PRINTED AND PUBLISHED WEEKLY, FOR THE CHURCH OF JESUS CHRIST OF LATTER DAY SAINTS.

TERMS:

TWO DOLLARS PER ANNUM, PAYABLE, INVARIABLY, IN ADVANCE.

All letters and communications must be directed to JAMES J. STRANG, *post paid*, or they will not be taken from the post office.

EXISTENCE OF GOD.

MR. BURGESS TO MR. STRANG.—No. 8.

Racine, May 7th, 1849.

MR. JAMES J. STRANG:—In reply to your third review of my third letter, par. 205, I still think weighing the hog proves the testimony true or false ; for if " testimony proved the fact," why do we demonstrate by weighing?

185. You ask, par. 206, " whence originated this principle in weights, this standard to which all weights must conform?" You say the authority established it. But what established the authority? Is not the authority derived from the people by their delegates? In despotism authority may be usurped by force. Among the superstitious a pretended revelation might suffice. But with a free and enlightened people, authority must be the expression of their will. Succeeding generations may recognize the same standard, till they discover a better. But the authority will still be founded on their agreement. You speak of " authority " as the opinion of some great officer, and yet you tell me there is a natural impossibility in making an issue between testimony and authority. Why, they are so frequently in opposition, that I should be puzzled to know whether they agree or differ most.

186. You say, par. 207, you know of no greater dupe than he who thinks nobody honest, wise or true but himself. For once we agree. You continue, "and gives precedence to the common thief over the learned professions." I spoke of the " quacks," not the " learned," and should prefer your correspondence with less plagiarism. To return the compliment, if Mr. Strang prefers the company of " quacks" and plagiarists, I do not.

187. In reply to par. 209, when you can show a proposition which is self-evident or evident in itself, but not evident to yourself, or myself, or some other self, I shall be glad to learn the distinction. And when you can show anything which is perceptible to the eye and not to the mind, I will certainly own beat. Such distinctions quite overpower my comprehension.

188. You ask, " what is it to prove by demonstration, but to demonstrate by proof?" Par. 211. If you are really sincere when you say, "you confess yourself annoyed by such nonsense," why do you say testimony proves the fact? which is but saying that testimony testifies the fact. Our own nonsense does not seem so troublesome to us as that of others, probably from being more used to it, or in blissful ignorance of it.

    " Oh wad some power the giftie gie us,
    To see ourselves as others see us."

So says Burns. Do the priests, " who know how to avoid these expressions, know too much to debate at all?" It appears to me a pitiful way of lengthening a debate to cavil at common expressions,

in which the question at issue is not involved. A chemist says he will prove a fact in chemistry, which he demonstrates, and then claims he has proved it by demonstration. I will be silent if I find nothing more objectionable than that to reply to.

189. You say, par. 213, " the rotundity of the earth is demonstrated by the testimony of great numbers of witnesses." I cannot even now believe, notwithstanding your high authority, that the rotundity of the earth or the existence of God can by any possibility be demonstrated by testimony ; else demonstration and testimony are synonymous, and you again utter that " nonsense " of which you complain in me.

190. In par. 216 you boast your extensive acquaintance with all kinds of society, a majority of whom profess to have seen and received communications from the supernatural. How does this agree with par. 86, where, speaking of spirits, you say, I am not aware that in any true sense they are supernatural? If, as you admit, there is nothing really supernatural, but only portions of nature relatively fine, which cannot govern the whole themselves, being parts, and subject to the governing influence of other parts, I think the point in issue is decided. You admit all I claim, that all the phenomena we witness are natural, and the different portions of nature mutually govern each other. If not, pray tell me how to distinguish the natural from the supernatural. I have asked the question so often in vain, that I am without hope of obtaining an answer.

191. In par. 223 you say you cannot distinguish between the natural and the supernatural, except by the popular distinction, or by saying that which is highest is super. Query. What is the standard of the highest? The difficulty still remains. And what the " popular distinction " is, I cannot even guess.

192. You say, par. 216, speaking of the Mormon doctrine, " it is believed by those who examine its evidence, because they cannot fail to appreciate its evidences," unless they are deeply interested in opposition. This might be said by the advocates of all kinds of superstition or notions, true or false, without helping us to perceive their truth or falsehood. However, having no vested interest in opposition to Mormonism, unless my aversion to being duped by priests be considered such, I shall be happy to examine the evidences at our leisure, if you desire to advance them. For this reason I stated in the opening of our discussion, that " my denial extended to the existence of the supernatural, and the revelation of his will in any written form whatever."

193. You say, par. 220, you " have exposed the absurdity of my grounds of doubt, by showing that the most certain facts in history and science are no better proved, and as much doubted." This only shows how little reason we have to believe those things called facts in history and science, and is good evidence for doubt instead of belief. If I desired to govern the credulous with my notions, I would advance such arguments as you do. But if I wished them to be governed by truth, I would encourage them to inquire continually concerning it. In fine, to do their own thinking, and let the priests do their own working, and thus make the minds and bodies of both more efficient for the promotion of happiness to the race, and less liable to be dupes or slaves. Yours for the truth,

EDWIN BURGESS.

KING STRANG'S ARREST.

While visiting a brother in the city of Detroit, President Millard Fillmore was informed that among the remote islands of Lake Michigan a person named Strang had established what he termed a kingdom, but what actually was but a nest of freebooters engaged in robbing the mails and counterfeiting the coin. The president dispatched the armed steamer Michigan to the insular kingdom, and ordered the arrest of the king for treason. The Michigan reached the harbor of St. James one midnight. The next morning the King went aboard and surrendered himself, as did two score other Mormons. The officers had been told that in an artificial cavern in Mount Pisgah the workshop of the counterfeiters could be found. They failed to locate such a cave.

After holding a court under an awning on the steamer's deck and taking a mass of testimony, the United States officials released many of the Mormons and steamed for Detroit with King Strang and a few of his leading men. There, from the latter part of May till the 9th of July, was held a trial that attracted attention all over the country. The indictments against Strang were on twelve counts, including mail robbery, counterfeiting and treason. He conducted his own defense with such skill and shrewdness as to result in his acquittal. His speech to the jury was highly dramatic. He pictured himself a martyr to religious persecution. He was a master of emotional oratory, and on this occasion particularly so. His acquittal was gained in the face of a violent local prejudice and the most virulent attacks in the local press. It was a victory that gave him an immense prestige at home, and aided him abroad.

Biding his opportunity, Strang planned to secure the machinery of the law in his own hands. He so shrewdly manipulated politics that the solid vote of Beaver Island became of great concern to politicians. To the discomfiture of the people of Mackinac, in 1851, the Mormons elected all the county officers. They now had the sheriff and the entire machinery of law, and could do as they pleased. A Mormon sheriff could serve the warrants, a Mormon jury convict and a Mormon judge sentence anyone resisting the mandate or authority of the King. In 1853 King Strang secured his own election to the legislature by clever political manipulation. His candidacy was not announced until election day; the Mormons then plumped their votes for him and snowed under their unsuspecting enemies, who supposed their own candidate would go in without an opposing candidate. An attempt was made to prevent Strang from taking his seat by serving an old warrant for his arrest. To outwit his foes Strang barricaded himself in his stateroom and withstood a siege till the boat entered the St. Clair, when he broke down the door and sought neutral territory by jumping on a wharf on the Canadian shore. Arrived at the capital, he ascertained that his seat would be contested. He argued his own case, and made such a favorable impression that he obtained the disputed seat. As a legislator he proved industrious and tactful, so that at the close of the session the Detroit Advertiser said of him:

"Mr. Strang's course as a member of the present legislature has disarmed much of the prejudice which had previously surrounded him. Whatever may be said or thought of the peculiar sect of which he is the local head, throughout this session he has conducted himself with a degree of decorum and propriety which have been equaled by his industry, sagacity, good temper, apparent regard for the true interests of the people, and the obligations of his official oath."

THE RULE OF THE KING.

During this period of his reign the power of King Strang was at its zenith. Among his own people his word was law, and those outside the fold dared not say him nay. He was

monarch of all he surveyed, and he proceeded to put into effect
ideas which he had long treasured.   The use of intoxicants was
prohibited, and likewise of coffee, tea and tobacco.   There was
a code that strictly governed all morals and religious observ-
ance, and violations were punished with a rigor that forbade
repetition.   Tithes were required of every husbandman, and
the firstling of every flock and the first fruits of the harvest
went to the royal storehouse.   Schools were established, and
from the royal press were issued books and pamphlets in great
number, all of them the product of Strang's prolific pen.   The
Northern Islander was published weekly and then daily.
Nothing escaped the watchful eye of the King, whose capacity
for work seemed equal to every demand.   He was a busy pam-
phleteer, and he wrote long letters to the papers of the east
defending his people against the accusations leveled at them.
The Smithsonian Institute found in him a contributor; his
paper upon the "Natural History of Beaver Island" was
printed in its ninth annual report.

In his government of the island King Strang developed a
marvelous capacity for detail.   This found expression in an
autocratic sway that dictated not only the ecclesiastical cus-
toms of his subjects, but everything connected with their daily
life.   Women were required to wear bloomers; men were
required to be as decorous in their conduct as women; gaming
was prohibited as strictly as was the use of intoxicants and
narcotics.   About this time, also, the doctrine of plural marriages was openly advocated; it had been tentatively broached
several years before.   Polygamy never made much headway,
despite the example set by the King, who enlarged his family
by taking five wives.   It is asserted that not more than twenty
plural marriages took place on the island..

While seemingly securely entrenched, the Mormon kingdom was at this time really crumbling.   From time to time
malcontents had been bred among the King's subjects, and

they joined the hostile fishermen on the small islands and on the mainland opposite. King Strang conceived a brilliant plan to bring them back to allegiance or suffer the penalty of his displeasure. A grand jury was called to meet at St. James; some of these men were to be summoned as jurors and some as witnesses. The Mormon sheriff and his posse went to Charlevoix (Pine River) to serve a summons on one Savage, who had been an elder and had incurred Strang's displeasure.[31] Savage read the summons, tore the paper into shreds and stamped his heel upon the fragments. As the sheriff laid his hand on the shoulder of Savage to arrest him, the latter gave a signal. There was an answering shout, and a score of sturdy fisher lads came running to the rescue. The Mormons hastily ran for their boats. A pursuing volley wounded two of them, but the party managed to put off in their boat. The fishermen also tumbled into boats, and then ensued a race for life. The Mormons struggled at the oars in desperation, as the bullets whistled over them or pierced the sides of the boat, while hard behind came the avengers intent on their death. Off in the distance could be seen the bellowed sails of a vessel, and for this the Mormons made as their only hope. Bleeding and spent, they managed to reach the craft before their pursuers could overtake them, and appealed to the captain to save them. It chanced that the sailor was a humane man, and he gave them shelter and refused to yield to the demand of the pursuers that the Mormons be turned over to them.[32]

King Strang at once took steps to punish the colonists at Charlevoix, but they had taken the alarm and fled. The Mormons erected a lofty gallows and adorned it with this inscription:

"THE MURDERERS OF PINE RIVER."

Another serious encounter occurred when a Mormon constable attempted to arrest Thomas and Samuel Bennett, Gen-

---

[31] See appendix, narrative of Ludlow P. Hill.

[32] See appendix, narrative of the rescue by Capt. E. S. Stone.

tiles who lived on Beaver Island. They resisted; Thomas
Bennett was instantly shot dead and his brother had one hand
nearly shot away.

ASSASSINATION OF THE KING.

Such episodes caused renewed activity in the Gentile
strongholds among those who planned to sweep the Mormon
settlements with fire and sword. Before their plans could be
executed the King was assassinated by two of his rebellious

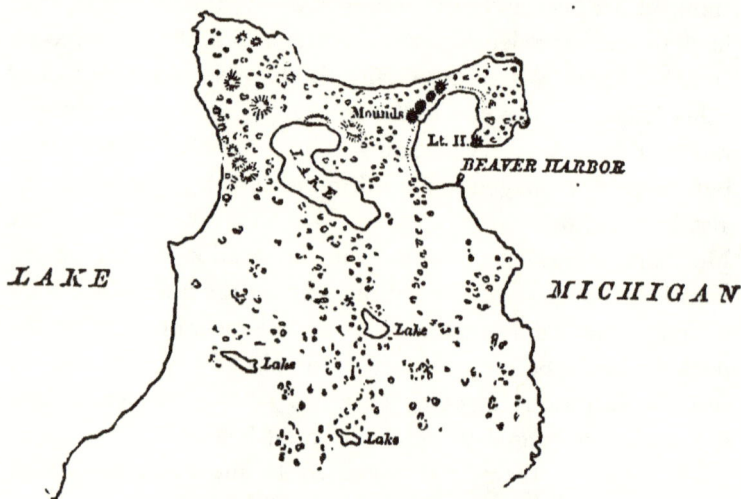

NORTHERN END OF BEAVER ISLAND.
(From the Smithsonian Report for 1878.)
Showing the harbor of St. James and the mounds whereon the Mormon temple
and public buildings of the kingdom were erected.

subjects—Thomas Bedford and Alexander Wentworth. Bedford had been whipped by order of the King for some offense;
he is said to have upheld his wife in disregarding the mandate
to wear bloomers. Wentworth also had a grievance. About
the middle of June, 1856, the Michigan steamed into the harbor, and by invitation of the captain King Strang proceeded to
visit the vessel's officers. As he was about to step on the pier,
two pistol shots were fired from behind, both taking effect. He

turned and recognized the assassins as they fired again.   As he sank to the ground they struck him over the head and face with the weapons, ran aboard the steamer and gave themselves up. They were taken to Mackinac, where the murderers were received as heroes.   They were never brought to trial.

The wounds of Strang proved fatal.   He called his elders to his deathbed, gave them instructions for the government of his Mormon kingdom, and as a last request asked to be taken to the city of refuge which he had founded in Wisconsin.   There he died July 9, 1856, and there his bones rest in an unmarked grave.

The kingdom fell with him.   The Gentile invasion came soon after his removal to Voree.   The fishermen came with torch to destroy and with ax to demolish.   The printing office was sacked; the tabernacle was reduced to ashes; the Mormons were exiled.   On the islands of Green Bay and its adjacent peninsula a few of them built new homes; some sought the land whence they had followed their prophet; the rest were scattered to the four points of the compass.   Like that of the prophet Joseph, the life of the prophet James ended in a tragedy and the exile and dispersion of his people.[33]

HENRY E. LEGLER.

May 11, 1897.

---

[33] Strang was survived by his five wives. Four of his twelve children were born after his death, one being born to each of his polygamous wives.

APPENDIX.

I.

· STRANG'S AUTOBIOGRAPHY.

Following is a copy of a writing found among the papers of James Jesse Strang after his death:

I was born March 21st, 1813, on Popple Ridge road, town of Scipio, Cayuga county, New York. My infancy was a period of continual sickness and extreme suffering, and I have understood that at one time I was so low as to be thought dead, and that preparations were made for my burial. All my early recollections are painful, and at this day I am utterly unable to comprehend the feeling of those who look back with pleasure on their infancy, and regret the rapid passing away of childhood. Till I had children of my own, happy in their infantile gambols, the recollection of those days produced a kind of creeping sensation akin to terror.

My parentage was decidedly respectable. My father is a descendant of Henry de l' Estrange, who accompanied the Duke of York to the new world to conquer the Dutch colony of New Amsterdam, now the State of New York, and the family has ever since retained an honorable rank, and is now scattered over nearly all the States, and branches of it are found in British America and the West Indies.

Tradition says they originally settled at New Utrecht, on Long Island, but Henry de l' Estrange, before his death, removed to the town of Rye, Westchester County, New York, where some of his descendants remained till since 1840.

Tradition also says that my great-grandfather accompanied the first English expedition to Michilimackinac, during which he contracted a dangerous sickness, that he was sent back for medical treatment, and died on the way from the residence of Sir William Johnson to Albany.

He left two sons, William and Gabriel, who were brought up among their mother's relatives, and by that means became separated from the family. They settled at a very early period at Stillwater, in Saratoga County, New York, and were lost sight of by the Strangs in the south part of New York, and on numerous genealogical trees found in that country the limb breaks off with their names.

My father, Clement Strang, is the fifth son of Gabriel Strang. Coming originally of a Norman stock who have continually intermarried with the Dutch and German families of the Hudson, he partakes (as I do) more of the German type than any other. Counting continually in the male line for ten generations back, our ancestors are Jews, but so large is the admixture of other blood that the Semitic type seems to be quite lost.

My mother is of the purest Yankee stock from Rhode Island, her father, Jesse James, and her grandfather, James James, having left there about the time of her birth, and settled in Greenfield, Saratoga County, New York, where they died full of years and honors.

My father and mother are yet living (1855), with a reasonable prospect that they may remain many years. They are both small of stature, my father being only five feet three or four inches, and mother less; of comely appearance, amiable, affectionate, charitable, remarkably industrious, skillful in labor and judicious in business, and unsullied moral and religious character. I have a brother, David Strang, two years older than myself, and a sister, Myraette Loser, five years younger, and it is a great pleasure to know that there has never been a disagreement to amount to so much as a momentary coldness between any two members of the family.

I learn from many sources that in childhood I exhibited extraordinary mental imbecility. Indeed, if I may credit what is told me on the subject, all who knew me, except my parents, thought me scarcely more than idiotic. Several facts remain in my recollection which support this opinion. I well recollect that school teachers not unfrequently turned me off with little or no attention, as though I was too stupid to learn and too dull to feel neglect, and my school fellows did not forget to add their slight.

I doubt not my appearance at least justified this opinion. I remember myself as little disposed to play, seldom cheerful, and scarcely ever taking the slightest interest in the plays of others. Long weary days I sat upon the floor, thinking, thinking, thinking! occasionally asking a strange, uninfantile question and never getting an answer. My mind wandered over fields that old men shrink from, seeking rest and finding none till darkness gathered thick around and I burst into tears and cried aloud, and with a voice scarcely able to articulate told my mother that my head ached.

During the first and part of the second year of my life my father's residence was in that part of Scipio now included in Ledyard. He left for Manlius in August, 1815, when I was about seventeen months old, and with a singular tenacity of memory I kept that place so perfectly in memory that after twenty years' absence I was able to recognize the location in riding through.

To the present time the recollections of my mother carrying me in her arms, nursing me, and conversing with her sister about me, and of the road along which they walked, and the work going on by the roadside, is as distinct as the events of yesterday. It is the brightest of the few bright spots of my childhood, the only recollection of long years not accompanied with a sensation of pain.

Until 1816 my parents remained in Manlius, my father carrying on the farm of Mr. Fleming, an extensive farmer from Maryland, who also kept a very popular tavern on the Great Western turnpike. I have very few recollections of that period beyond an ill-defined but strong attachment to several members of his family and several of the colored people he brought there, though I have seen very few of them in forty years, and none of them in thirty-two. Such are the affections of childhood; at least, they are such with me.

In February, 1816, my father removed with his family to Hanover, Chautauqua County, New York, where he remained twenty years. His first location was two miles northeast of Forestville, and three-fourths of a mile from Walnut Creek, on the east side of the road, at the four corners, but a few years of the latter portion of that period we lived on Walnut Creek flats, in the same neighborhood.

There I grew up, and around that place cluster nearly all the recollections, pleasant and painful, of my childhood and youth.

On our journey I remember Buffalo as a small, straggling village of thirty or forty houses, occupied as taverns and drinking shops; so crowded that it was a matter of favor to get entertainment; where the same low, open, filthy room was used for barroom, dining room and kitchen, and a few hours the latter part of the night accommodated as many drowsy, drunken and tired sleepers as could lie down upon the floor.

From Buffalo we went to the mouth of Cattaraugus Creek on the ice. Father was heavy loaded and obliged to travel slow. There had been a day or two of mild weather; the snow was melted on the ice and had already thawed many a treacherous opening, and covered with water as the ice was, it was difficult for a stranger to keep the way over the thirty miles of dreary waste of ice without a landmark.

To secure a passage by daylight father got a man who was going with a two-horse sleigh and no load but his wife to take my mother and her two children as far as Cattaraugus. I only remember that the water sometimes came into the sleigh box, that the driver frequently jumped the horses across wide chasms in the ice, and sometimes found them so wide that he dare not cross them and went great distances around, and that my mother was terribly frightened, and hugged my brother and I to her with an almost suffocating grasp.

I have since I was grown up frequently heard her speak of that passage as having terrified her almost to distraction, a terror much heightened by the continual quarrels and mutual profanity of the couple with whom we rode.

We lost sight of father immediately after starting, and next saw him at Mack's tavern, Cattaraugus. The wind got into the northwest the afternoon of the day we started, and towards night one of the worst snowstorms of that latitude came on, obliterating in a few minutes every vestige of track on the ice, filling the air so that a man could not see the length of sled and team, and rendering it utterly impossible to keep a course even for a few rods.

This storm overtook father midway in the lake, about twenty miles above Buffalo. What he suffered and how he survived none can know, only those who have experienced a similar catastrophe.

I only remember that my mother cried incessantly, and ever and anon clasped my brother and myself convulsively in her arms, till three days passed, when he came to us as one from the dead. Several reports of his death had reached us, some by persons who had seen his frozen body. Whether some persons had really perished and been mistaken for him, or the reports were wholly false, I do not know, but the former is probable.

From Cattaraugus to my father's place in the same town was then two day's travel, though on an air line not six miles. The route was by Sheridan Center and Forestville.

1 attended school the following summer where the most moderate qualifications for teaching were satisfactory. There were but two scholars who knew the alphabet, and none who spelled "easy words of two syllables."

From this time till I was twelve years old I attended district school more or less every year, but the terms were usually short, the teachers inexperienced and ill qualified to teach, and my health such as to preclude attentive study or steady attendance. I estimate my attendance during the whole period as equal to six months' steady attendance with health for study.

My parents had good government. Their family were raised without beating. I can remember being very slightly whipped by my father twice and my mother once. My sister was raised without ever suffering chastisement either at home or in school, and my brother's fortune——

[Here the writing ends as if the writer had been disturbed, and never afterward had opportunity to resume the work.]

Copied January 27, 1897.

CHAS. J. STRANG,
Lansing, Mich.

II.

NARRATIVE OF LUDLOW P. HILL.

In his book on "Ancient and Modern Michilimackinac," Strang refers to "a disaffected family by the name of Hill." The writer became acquainted with a member of this family, Ludlow P. Hill, during the summer of 1896, while sojourning in the picturesque region along the east shore of Green Bay. Mr. Hill was induced, after much persuasion, to give his recollections of the Beaver Island community. Though sixty-six years of age, his memory was remarkably clear, and his narrative was told in a straightforward manner. Mr. Hill is at present a resident of Wonewoc, Wis. Following narrative was transcribed from the notes taken at the time of the interview:

When I went to Beaver Island I was a young man, who had just reached my majority. My family lived in Illinois (Elgin), and it was there that my father became acquainted with Strang and was deeply impressed with his remarkable powers. Strang induced him to join his Beaver Island colony and to invest his entire possessions there (about $10,000). That is how I came to go there, and all the rest of the family, too. I was the only member of the family who remained outside the Mormon fold, and was the last Gentile on the island who resisted the authority of King Strang. In fact, I was the last Gentile on the island, but I had to leave, too, for my life was threatened and my stay was made uncomfortable in many ways. It was not merely a secretly conveyed intimation that my departure would add to my personal comfort; I was denounced openly and by name in the tabernacle.

My father found out the charlatanism of Strang soon after reaching the island. Near the southern end of the island (the head) was a splendid property known to the Gentiles as the Cable property, but rechristened Galilee by the Saints owing to the resemblance, fancied or otherwise, of a small lake on the property to the body of water known to biblical readers. This geographical naming in adaptation of Bible places was a favorite one with the Mormons. Enoch was a small cluster of houses near the bay, and west of St. James was a ridge of sand dignified into Mount Pisgah. Lake Galilee was one-fourth mile from the beach and was remarkably deep for an inland lake.

When my father joined the Beaver Islanders, Strang had been carefully nursing his colony for some time, and felt strong enough to assume the airs, if not the title of dictator, as he later did of King. When my father had located, he was informed that the place he had bought would be managed by another Mormon, who would conduct it for the benefit of the community. He was coolly informed that this other man, who stood

close to Strang, had more business ability. To resist 'the
mandate seemed sheer folly to my father, for it meant ruin.
Nobody would have bought him out, because no Gentiles
would venture into a nest of pirates, as they regarded the
Mormons, and the Mormons, of course, would not buy him
out—they preferred to freeze him out. Without their consent
nobody could carry on any business. It was the boycott
refined to a point of absolute perfection and success. In those
days I was hot-blooded and stubborn, and I wasn't going to
give up so easily. So I determined to bid defiance to Strang
and his crowd. I had secured the appointment of lighthouse
keeper and decided to stick to my post at all hazards. The
place paid very poorly—I think not to exceed $500 per
annum—but even this was coveted by the Mormons, who were
determined upon complete control of the island and everything
on it. And they made it hot enough for me, I assure you.
Had I consented to be baptized and to join the fold, it would
have been pleasant enough, but as I have said, there was a
grain of stubbornness about me that made me hot-headed and
defiant. I need not give in detail the devices that were
employed to make my lot far from hum-drum. I will only
narrate one instance. Orders came to me from the King's
men that under no circumstances must I harbor any Gentiles,
or there would be trouble. Early one raw morning there
came to the beach in a leaky boat a couple of half-frozen and
half-starved fishermen, who had been wave-tossed in a heavy
sea for several days, and asked food and shelter.

"It's as much as your life is worth," said I, "to be caught
here, and maybe I would fare as bad if I helped you. I'll give
you a bite to eat, though, but you had better not stop any
longer than necessary, for the Mormons may be here any
minute."

When they heard this I didn't need to hurry them a bit; they
didn't even want to stop for something to eat, until I urged

them to do so. They had put out into the lake but a short time
when there came in hot haste to the door six or seven of the
guard, armed with guns and demanding if I had seen any Gentiles, or if I had given them any comfort or aid. I deemed it
prudent to buy safety at the expense of veracity, and they left
vowing that if they caught the men, whose boat they had
descried from a distance as it was coming to shore, they would
make short work of the intruders.

I married a Mormon young woman, and I may say I have
never regretted the step. All of her family were Mormons,
and they and my father's family (all Mormons except myself)
were among those who did not fall into polygamous ways on
the island. Yes, we were married under rather unusual circumstances, and I got the best of the King, the deputy King
(vice King), the King's council, and all the elders, too. (Mr.
Hill chuckled as the narration called up slumbering recollections.) Yes, I'll tell you how it was, and it's the truth, too.
The Mormons were always willing to marry a Gentile woman
to a Mormon man, figuring that they could bring enough influence to bear on the woman to attach her and her children to the
church. But when it came to uniting a Gentile man with a
Mormon girl, they were inexorable in their refusal. We knew
that, of course, and Cecelia (that's my wife's name) urged me to
be baptized and thus overcome the difficulty.

"Cecelia," said I, "I think the world of you, but a Mormon
I'll never consent to become, and that doesn't mean, either, that
we won't be married. I'll find some other way."

Now, although I was a Gentile, and one whom the ruling
powers were only biding their time to get out of the way, I had
a good many friends among the Mormons. So I bided my
time. I may mention here that Strang, with his usual shrewdness, had, in order to carry out his schemes under forms of law,
brought about the organization of the County of Emmet, to
include Beaver Island, and thus had control of the whole

machinery of county government. Thus he could elect a Mormon sheriff, and arrest people as he chose; could try his prisoners before a Mormon jury, and a Mormon judge would sentence them according to Mormon law. So every one whom he didn't like became an outlaw, of course, for he had no difficulty in trumping up charges. Strang also got himself elected as a member of the legislature, where he could get local laws passed for Beaver Island. When he went to Lansing as a member of the legislature, he left his kingdom in charge of the president of his council. I waited till Strang had gone to Lansing for the winter, and then I proceeded to put my plans into execution. It had been suspected, despite our precautions, that Cecelia and myself were attached to each other, so I went to one of the preachers whom I regarded as friendly—a man named Aldrich—and asked him to marry us. He looked startled and said he wouldn't think of such a thing. Finally he said he would if I would consent to be baptized. I flatly declined this proposition. Then he said:

"I'll go and see Bacon," (he was the president of the council and his word was law when Strang was away). "I think I can induce him to give his consent."

Aldrich jumped into his sleigh and drove to the King's house. He was gone some time, and when he came back I saw at once that his mission had been fruitless. Bacon had positively refused to consent to the marriage.

It was evident that I must get at it in another way. There was another Mormon elder and preacher—one Savage—whose friendship I had won, and I went to him. I told him the circumstances and asked him whether he would tie the knot for us.

"It would be ruin to me," said he.

Now, I knew that for some time Savage had been disaffected, so I took the cue from that and worked at him till I persuaded him to perform the ceremony secretly. You may be sure that this was no easy matter, either, and I swore by all that was holy that under no circumstances would I betray him as long as there was danger to him in so doing. So after he had given his word, we planned how we would do it.

The young people of the colony had arranged for a party to be given at my father's house on a certain evening, and we arranged that this circumstance should be taken advantage of to consummate our plans. You see we had to plan, for we were watched. It was a cold, clear starlight night. I remember it well, although it was more than fifty years ago. Within the house all was gaiety and noise—the sound of the fiddle, the patter of the dancers' shoes and the laughter of the merry young people. By a prearrangement, Cecelia and two of our friends who were in the secret repaired to a room up-stairs, while I went outdoors. In the shadow of a woodpile near by Elder Savage was awaiting my signal. He cautiously made his way to the house, went up by a rear stairway, and I followed. In that up-stairs room, while below there was playing and dancing and laughter, Cecelia and I were united in marriage. Not a member of my family or of my wife's family was present or knew anything about it. The reason for keeping them ignorant I'll tell you later. Only my wife and I, the preacher and our two witnesses—friends whom we trusted implicitly, and who, besides, would keep still to save themselves from the vengeance of the Church, if for no other reason, were present. The ceremony over, we went down one at a time without exciting comment, the elder making his exit unobserved, and entering the house an hour later as if he had just arrived to take part in the festival of the young people.

That is how we were secretly married. To the neighbors we behaved just as before. Cecelia received the attentions of other young men, and I was devoted to two or three other women. But there was one present whom we couldn't hoodwink. She was afterwards one of Strang's wives. She was a remarkably clever young woman, if she did play me a mean trick. This young woman was well educated. On one occasion when Strang went east on a proselyting tour, this young woman accompanied him as his secretary, dressed as a young man. They visited Philadelphia, New York and other large cities, and the deception of her sex was never discovered. Well, this young woman acted as a spy on us, and by eavesdropping learned the facts about our marriage. She revealed it all to the King's men, and Savage was summoned to appear. He came to me in great alarm.

"We are lost. They know everything," said he. "I am a ruined man."

Now, I had sworn when he promised to perform the secret ceremony that I would protect him at all hazards. So I set my brains to work and I unfolded a plan to him for getting out of the scrape. I had heard that King Strang had on one occasion secretly baptized a Gentile, so I said to Savage: "Tell them that you secretly baptized me before you performed the marriage ceremony, and if they won't accept that sort of a ceremony as valid, plead as justification that you followed the high example set by Strang."

The trial was a long drawn out affair. My parents were summoned. They truthfully said that they were as much surprised as anybody to hear that we were a married couple, not having been present or even apprised as to the ceremony. My brother gave the same testimony, which let them out from punishment. Until Elder Savage's turn came, the prosecution rested on the eavesdropping information obtained by Strang's future wife.

When it came to Savage's turn, he readily admitted having performed the marriage rites, and the drawn brows and black looks of the councillors were not cheerful premonitions of his fate. When he went on to tell, however, that he had not done so until he had baptized me a Mormon, there was a murmur of astonishment. Savage added that in doing so he had not erred, for he had but followed the example of the head of the community, who, of course, could do no wrong.

This was a poser for those who wanted to condemn Savage to the rigors of the Mormon canon. Though unconvinced, they could hardly convict Savage for doing what their own high priest had done; so Savage escaped punishment. He hadn't strictly told the truth, nor had I, but when men's lives and property are the issue, one doesn't view moral questions from the same standpoint as ordinarily.

But Savage did not feel safe. He secretly prepared for early departure, and early in the spring, with a few followers who were as discontented as himself with Mormon rule as expounded on Beaver Island, stole away in Mackinac boats. The refugees went to the main shore, building cabins on the site of the town of Charlevoix. Strang was not disposed to permit his prey to escape so easily.   His Mormon sheriff summoned a Mormon posse and went after the seceders on pretext of summoning them as jurors.   Thus, under cover of law, he could get his subject back to the island, where he could do whatever his vindictive spirit might suggest. Savage, of course, saw through the artifice. When the sheriff's posse appeared at his log hut with the warrant, Savage tore the paper into shreds, threw them under his feet and stamped on the fragments. The Mormon officers then tried to arrest him for resisting their lawful authority. Savage seized his gun, his companions hurried to his rescue with their weapons, and the Mormon officers turned tail and ran. A pursuing volley wounded one of them in the wrist and another in the groin. They managed to put out in their boat, pursued by their now thoroughly aroused assailants, but the opportune appearance of a vessel enabled them to escape by appealing to her captain for protection.

It was evident to Savage that to remain on the mainland opposite the island whence he had fled was to invite annihilation, for he knew Strang would never rest till he had hunted him down. The refugees placed their belonging and families aboard the steamer "Little Columbia," from Buffalo to Green Bay, and arranged to meet the boat beyond Beaver Island, after her departure from St. James. As usual, the steamer put into the harbor at St. James, and the Mormons crowded aboard. The families of the refugees kept close to their cabins and remained unobserved. All went well till one of the Mormons noticed the names on some of the boxes. At once there was great commotion, and the seizure of the vessel was ordered. The captain's promptness in getting out of the harbor prevented this.

In the meantime the male contingent had sailed around to the southern end of the island, and made a stop at my place. They were overjoyed to see me, and we told each other what had happened since last we had met. I proposed to the men a plan for the overthrow of the kingdom. If they hadn't lacked the nerve, the career of the prophet-king and his reign would have been cut short a few years sooner than it was. Near by in the woods were some seven or eight Mormons of the worst stripe engaged in cutting timber. I proposed that we sally forth, pick our men, surprise them and then shoot them down. As fast as others came we could serve them the same way, and if a large force should arrive, we could barricade ourselves in the house and pick off the men at leisure. I knew there were disaffected men in the community who would lead an uprising if they could get a good chance. I believed it practicable to thus overthrow the kingdom. But they wouldn't take the risk. They departed to join their families, and succeeded in doing so. On Washington Island, at the mouth of Green Bay, they made their homes, and some of their descendants live there to-day.

It was not long after this that I left Beaver Island. Events there were becoming rather too warm even for me. To entrap me into his net, Strang had me summoned as a grand juror immediately after Savage and his companions shot his officers. It was the first grand jury that ever met on Beaver Island. There I was placed in the position of voting to indict my best friends for doing something that grew directly out of circumstances brought about by myself. Of course, I didn't hesitate to do so. I knew the birds would be flown, and I didn't propose to fall into the pit dug for me. I saw, however, that it was dangerous to remain where I was, and I received numerous warnings of the fate that lay in store for me. Men had disappeared before, and no one was the wiser. Houses had gone up in smoke and there was no explanation of the origin of the flames. I quietly made my arrangements and silently hied me away.

Strang was in many respects a remarkable man. He was small and spare, but as a speaker he towered like a giant. He was one of the most fascinating orators imaginable. He wore a very heavy beard of reddish tinge, and his hair was red, too. He had dark eyes, that looked at one on occasion as though they could bore right through. They were set close together, under wide projecting brows, from which rose a massive forehead. Add to this a thin hatchet face, and you have a grouping of features that would attract attention anywhere. His oratory was of the fervid, impassioned sort that would carry his audience with him every time. His words came out in a torrent; he could work himself into emotional spells at will, the sincerity of his words being attested by tears when necessary to produce that effect, or by infectious laughter when his mood was merry. He had what is known as magnetism, too, and could be one of the most companionable of men. His influence over his followers was unbounded. He was certainly a man of unusual talents in many respects. Had he chosen to use them for good, he would have left a great impress upon his country. When I was a young lad I heard him in a debate with a Catholic speaker in Elgin, Ill. It was to have been a three-days' debate. The priest brought up a number of news-paper stories to confound his adversary. In reply Strang con-fined himself entirely to the Scriptures. He so thoroughly dis-comfited his adversary in the debate that the next evening the priest failed to appear, and the judges awarded the verdict to Strang.

III.

MRS. CECELIA HILL'S RECOLLECTIONS.

Personal recollections of Mrs. Cecelia Hill, wife of Ludlow P. Hill, in an interview during the summer of 1896:

My parents were Mormons who were captured by the oratory of Strang and followed him to Beaver Island. I was fifteen years old at the time. I was present when Strang was crowned King. The ceremony took place in the tabernacle, a building about eighty feet long, constructed of hewn logs and but partly completed at the time of the coronation. Like any young woman under similar circumstances, I was anxious to be present and managed to get into the tabernacle. At one end was a platform, and towards it marched the procession of elders and other quorums, escorting the King. First came the King, dressed in a robe of bright red, and accompanied by his council. Then followed the twelve elders, the seventy and the minor orders of the ministry, or quorums, as they were called. The people were permitted to occupy what space remained in the tabernacle.

The chief ceremonials were performed by Geo. J. Adams, president of the council of elders. Adams was a man of imposing presence. He was over six feet tall and he towered over the short-statured King, who, however, made up in intel-

lect what he lacked in frame. Adams had been an actor, and
he succeeded in making the crowning of the King a very
imposing ceremony. It ended by placing upon the auburn
head of Strang a crown of metal. The crown was a plain
circlet, with a cluster of stars projecting in front.

It was July 8th that this ceremony occurred, and every
recurring 8th of July was known as the King's Day and was
celebrated as a holiday with many festivities. The entire population of the island would gather at a place in the woods to go
through prescribed ceremonials—the hewers of wood and the
drawers of water to make proper obeisance to the King. There
were burnt offerings to begin with. The head of each family
brought a fowl and a heifer was thereupon killed. Its body
was dissected without breaking a bone. After these ceremonials there was feasting and rejoicing and the people danced on
the greensward. King's Day was the same with the islanders
as the Fourth of July is with us.

The Mormons under Strang strove to follow strictly the old
Mosaic law. Every man who went with Strang was given "an
inheritance." The tithing system was in full effect. The firstling of every flock and the first fruits of the orchard and the
field were due to the King's court. Every one who went into
the church was compelled to give as his first contribution one-
tenth of all his possessions. The people believed in the Mosaic
law implicitly, even to the stoning of a rebellious child. There
was a fisherman named Bennett, who resisted and wounded a
Mormon officer and was shot to death. In following out the
injunction to throw a stone upon the grave of any man guilty of
shedding the blood of the Saints, a pile of stones was heaped
upon his grave big enough for a monument. When the fishermen raided the island after Strang's death, they compelled the
Mormons to pick every one of these stones off the grave of
Bennett and cast them into the lake. Most of the subjects of
Strang were Americans, and many of them were sincere, earn-

est and intelligent. The head men were, I believe, imposters who sought to live off the labor of others. I have already mentioned Adams, the actor. He was chief in authority when Strang was away. Afterwards he became disgruntled and went into the prophet business on his own account. He led a band of Mormons to Africa and abandoned them there. After Adams left one Bacon was the King pro tem. Gen. Miller was the chief in military authority. He had been a bishop of the church at Nauvoo, and came with two wives. He married another one on the island—a young woman, although he was an old gray-haired man. I think Strang had five wives, and his death prevented his adding two more to the list—two sisters. His first wife's maiden name was Perse, his second Alvina Fields. His third we knew as Aunt Betsy,* and is, I believe, still living. When Chicago was destroyed by fire she said that "James prophesied it," and took it as a judgment for the persecution of her husband. She never lost faith in her husband.

IV.

THE BATTLE ON THE LAKE.

E. S. Stone was the captain of the bark aboard which Mormon fugitives sought refuge when pursued by the Gentile fishermen of Pine River. I am indebted to Col. George P. Mathes, of Milwaukee, for permission to use following narrative, dictated by Capt. Stone for the manuscript collection of Col. Mathes:

In the year 1852, while on my trip up from Buffalo to Chicago on the bark Morgan, in passing through the Straits of Mackinaw one very calm summer afternoon, when about half-way between Beaver Island and Pine River on the main land (south shore), and while at dinner in the cabin, we heard great firing of guns; and on rushing on deck, saw a small fleet of row-

*September 22, 1897.—While this paper is in press, the telegraphic news in the daily papers announces the death of "Aunt Betsy," the polygamous third wife of James Strang.

boats on the surface of the calm water coming toward our vessel from the south shore. They were evidently in a fierce battle, and viewing them through my spyglass, I saw that there were three Mackinaw boats filled with men fleeing from some larger barges, double banked with oars, that were rapidly gaining on the smaller boats, and firing on them as fast as they could load and fire. When the smaller boats got near enough to hail us, they asked us for God's sake to take them on board and save them from being murdered, as they were completely exhausted and could pull no longer and were being shot to pieces. Of course, common humanity compelled me to grant their request, and as they pulled alongside to be taken on board, the bullets flying thick about them, and some striking the bows of the vessel as they pulled behind it, the boats in chase hailed me, demanding that I should drive them off, as they were Mormons, robbers and thieves, and they wanted to kill every one of them; and if I did not do so they would fire into my vessel, which threat I knew they dared not carry out. In taking the Mormons on board, I found all of them armed with rifles, and the first one as he stepped on board turned and said: "Now, we will give it to them." I caught and disarmed him and all the rest as they came over the rail. When they were all on board I asked the fishermen from Pine River to come nearer and talk with me, which they did, but not near enough to be recognized, as there were some on both sides that knew me and called me by name. The fishermen claimed that the Mormons were the aggressors, which the Mormons denied, saying they had not fired a shot, and showed me their guns were all loaded. I found that out of the fifteen Mormons that were in the Mackinaw boats, eight were severely wounded, their boats were riddled with bullets and bespattered with blood, and the water in the bottom of the boats very bloody; and it seemed almost a miracle that none of them were killed.

An oar pulled by one of them was struck by three bullets, yet the man was unhurt.

The fishermen laid by on their oars for some time watching us, and finally, when they got tired of waiting for the Mormons to leave the vessel, pulled back to their home at Pine River. We dressed the wounds of the Mormons the best we could and fed them, and at night, under cover of the darkness, they got into their boats and pulled for their homes on Beaver Island.

When I arrived in Chicago I gave to a reporter rather a burlesque account of a sea fight between the "Latter Day Saints" and the "Gentiles," which was not much relished by King Strang. However, the Mormons as a body were very grateful for their rescue, and later in the fall, when I was obliged to run into Beaver Harbor for safety in a storm, they gave a ball and banquet in my honor, and I led the first dance with King Strang's favorite wife. The women were all dressed in calico bloomers, and the costumes of the men were equally odd and conspicuous.

There had long been bad blood between the Mormons and the Gentiles, and this particular battle was caused by the setting off of a new county in what was then called Northern Michigan, including Beaver Island, many other islands, Mackinaw, and nearly a hundred miles of the south shore. In organizing the county and electing its officers the Mormons had held an election on Beaver Island and elected their officers, claiming that as the county seat, while the Gentiles had held an election at Mackinaw and elected their officers, and claimed a legal election and the county seat. At this time the Mormon county judge had issued a mandamus, or something of the kind, for a grand jury, and claimed the jurors were drawn from different parts of the county and had been summoned to appear at Beaver Island, which they had failed to do, and the Mormon sheriff had been ordered to go over to the main land with this posse and arrest the jurors and bring them over to Beaver

Island. When they reached Pine River and began to make the arrests, they resisted and the fight commenced. The Gentiles claimed that the "Latter Day Saints," finding them too much for them, fired and ran, and took to their boats, and got such a start before they got organized and in their boats that they were first able to reach the Morgan and save their lives. But the war still continued after this encounter, until the Mormons, getting the worst of it, appealed to the United States government for protection, and the frigate Michigan was sent to remove all the Mormons from Beaver Island to Wisconsin. When they got there some renounced the faith and some imigrated to Salt Lake, and King Strang had not enough of a following to organize a new community, and I do not remember what finally became of him.

E. S. STONE,

By MRS. STONE.

P. S.—Mr. Stone has been very ill, but being much better, yet not quite equal to writing, has dictated this to me and I have written it in haste.

MRS. E. L. STONE.

V.

INTERVIEW WITH JUDGE LYON.

Interview with Judge William Penn Lyon, of the Wisconsin Supreme Court:

I lived at Burlington and knew Strang well. He was an eccentric man, but a shrewd and able one in many respects. How he drew so many men of intelligence under his influence is one of the strange circumstances which we know to be, but can not explain. I have no doubt most of his converts were sincere—they would hardly have given up all they possessed otherwise. My partner Barnes always believed Strang to be sincere, too, and he was a man of intelligence and penetration. Strang converted some of the best people of Burlington to Mormonism. Among them I may mention Wm. Aldrich,

whose son has since served a term or two in the legislature;
Hale, whose son became eminent as a geologist, and Titus G.
Fish.

VI.

THE BURIED PLATES OF LABAN.

From the "Revelations of James J. Strang," as compiled by
Wingfield Watson, of Spring Prairie:

(Revelation given to James J. Strang, September 1, 1845.)

1. The angel of the Lord came unto me, James, on the
first day of September, in the year eighteen hundred and forty-
five, and the light shined about him above the brightness of the
sun, and he showed unto me the plates of the sealed record, and
he gave into my hands the Urim and Thummin, and out of the
light came the voice of the Lord saying: "My servant James,
in blessing I will bless thee, and in multiplying I will multiply
thee, because I have tried thee and found thee faithful. Behold
my servant James, I am about to bless thee with a great blessing, which shall be to those that love me an immutable testimony, to those who know me not a stumbling block; but to
those who have known me and have turned their hearts from
me a rock of offense. Yea, let them beware, for shame and
destruction walk in their tracks, and their time abideth but not
long.

2. A work shall come forth, and the secrets of the past
shalt thou reveal. Yea, by little and little shalt thou reveal it,
according to the ability and faithfulness of my church and of
my servants whom I have placed above them. Behold the
record which was sealed from my servant Joseph, unto thee it is
reserved. Take heed that thou count it not a light thing, nor
exalt thyself, lest thou be stricken; for by myself I swear that
as thou servest my faithfully and comest not short, thou shalt
unlock the mysteries thereof which I have kept hid from the

world. Yea, as my servants serve me so shalt thou translate unto them.

3. But in their weakness I have not forgotten them. Go to the place which the angel of the presence shall show 'thee, and there shalt thou dig for the record of my people in whose possessions thou dwellest. Take with thee faithful witnesses, for in evil will the unfaithful speak of thee; but the faithful and true shall know that they are liars and shall not stumble for their words.

4. Speak thou unto the elders of my church and say unto them: Hear my voice, and harken unto my words, for they are true and faithful. Testify, testify unto all the saints. Testify, testify in all the world. He that rejecteth you, him will I reject in the day that I come in my kingdom. Testify, testify unto him who has received my word and turned away. Let him now return unto me, and obey and serve his God, lest he be smitten with a curse, and his children curse him, and his name be blotted out of the book of life.

5. Yea, those to whom I have revealed myself, let them hearken unto me now, lest they be cast off in the day of my indignation, lest the consuming fire of the day of trial burn them up. Yea, lest the second death make them his prey, and they be cast into the lake that burns with fire and brimstone.

6. Rejoice, ye holy, for the day of your deliverance is near, and the time of your exaltation is at hand. Faithful and true are my words, dividing the marrow from the bones and truth from rottenness. He that rejecteth them, will I reject when I come in my kingdom. And while I was yet in the spirit, the angel of the Lord took me away to the hill in the east of Walworth, against White River in Voree, and there he showed unto me the record, buried under an oak tree as large as the body of a large man. It was enclosed in an earthen casement, and buried in the ground as deep as to a man's waist; and I beheld it as a man can see a light stone in clear water; for I saw it by Urim

and Thummim, and I returned the Urim and Thummim to the angel of the Lord and he departed out of my sight.

(Translation of the Voree Record by the Prophet James, by Urim and Thummim, September 18, 1845, as revealed in the foregoing revelation.)

1. My people are no more. The mighty are fallen and the young slain in battle. Their bones bleached on the plain by the noonday shadow. The houses are leveled to the dust, and in the moat are the walls. They shall be inhabited. I have in the burial served them, and their bones in the death shade toward the sun's rising are covered. They sleep with the mighty dead, and they rest with their fathers. They have fallen in transgression and are not, but the elect and faithful there shall dwell.

2. The word hath revealed it. God hath sworn to give an inheritance to his people where transgressors perished. The word of God came to me while I mourned in the deathshade, saying, I will avenge me on the destroyer. He shall be driven out. Other strangers shall inhabit the land. I an ensign there will set up. The escaped of my people there shall dwell, when the flock disown the shepherd and build not on the rock.

3. The forerunner men shall kill, but a mighty prophet there shall dwell. I will be his strength, and he shall bring forth thy record. Record my words and bury it in the hill of promise.

4. The record of Rajah Manchore of Vorito.

VOREE PLATES.

(Description of one side of one of the Voree Plates.)

1st. An eye. The symbol of God, who is all-seeing: consequently it is called the all-seeing eye, and has been used as symbolical of the Deity in all countries, and in all ages of the world.

2d. The figure of a man down to the waist having a crown resembling a cap, and composed of radiating lines, on his head;

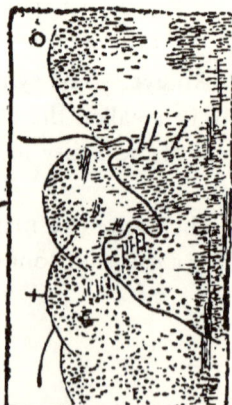

FACSIMILE OF CHARACTERS TRACED ON THE
VOREE PLATES.

and a scepter in his hand. These are symbols of authority, and shew him a ruler. As he has the sun, moon and stars (all the natural lights) below him, and only the all-seeing eye above him, he is prophet, seer, revelator, translator, and first president of the church—governing not by natural light, or mere human wisdom, but by revelation or the word of God, and derives his authority solely from God, and not in any sense from the actions of men.

3d. The sun on the right and the moon on the left. These represent the two vice-presidents, or counsellors in the first presidency; the two largest natural lights being used as symbols, because they are to assist the first president in wisdom, or natural light merely, and not by revelation.

4th. A cross pillar above and resting upon the center large star, and under the human figure, two pillars above and resting upon the two upper large stars, and below and between the sun and the moon. These represent coadjutors, assistants or helps, of whom there have been several since the beginning of the church, appointed by revelation.

5th. Twelve stars, six around the sun and six around the moon. These represent the High Council of the church. The division into classes of six each agrees with established usages in the church, one-half to stand up for the accuser, and the other for the accused. This is not the high council of the state.

6th. Twelve large stars. Ten of these in two rows at the bottom of the plate, and the other two over them, nearly between the sun and moon. They represent the twelve apostles. These stars are larger than those which represent the High Council of the Church, because the apostles have a more important ministry; but are placed below them because they are subject to their discipline, and below the symbols of the first presidency because they are subject to its directions.

7th. Seventy small stars immediately within the points of the twelve large ones, being six to each except the center one, which has only four. They represent the seventies, who are subject to the direction of the twelve apostles.

8th. A straight line dropping down before the scepter. "Therefore thus saith the Lord God, behold I lay in Zion for a foundation a stone, a tried stone, a precious corner stone, a sure foundation: he that believeth shall not make haste. Judgment also will I lay to the line and righteousness to the plummet; and the hail shall sweep away the refuge of lies, and the waters shall overflow the hiding place."

"Thus he shewed me; and behold the Lord stood upon a wall made by a plumb-line, with a plumb-line in his hand. And the Lord said unto me, Amos, what seest thou? And I said, a plumb-line. Then said the Lord, Behold I will set a plumb-line in the midst of my people Israel: I will not again pass by them any more."

These symbols were all prophetic of the order that will exist in the fullness of times. Thus God in His goodness to those who lived in days past has shown them not only the rest which He had in reservation for them, but the perfectness of the means by which He will accomplish it. Probably now we understand it in part, but in times to come we shall "know as we are known."

The Voree plates have disappeared. Chas. J. Strang writes concerning them: "I do not know where the plates are. I never saw them." Wingfield Watson writes: "The three Voree plates are in the hands of some one of Mr. Strang's family, whose address I do not now know."

VII.

STRANG'S BOOKS AND PAMPHLETS.

Owing to the destruction of the royal press at Beaver Island, by the torch, when the fishermen expelled the Mormons, copies of the books, pamphlets and newspapers published by King Strang are excessively scarce. Of the "Book of the Law of the Lord," Strang's most important book, there are probably not to exceed a dozen copies in existence. Chas. J. Strang, of Lansing; L. D. Hickey, of Coldwater, Mich.; Wingfield Watson, of Spring Prairie, Wis., and the writer each possess one. A copy is to be found in each of following libraries: Congressional, Washington, D. C.; State Library of Michigan, Lansing; Wisconsin Historical Society's Library, Madison.

Not one complete file of the "Northern Islander" or "Voree Herold" is known to be in existence. The latter comprised five volumes, issued the first year as a monthly and afterwards weekly. Its name was changed subsequently to "Gospel Herald" and "Zion's Reveille." A partial set is owned by the Wisconsin Historical Society, and a few scattering copies are owned respectively by Chas. J. Strang and the writer. The paper was published at Voree, Wis., from 1846 to 1850. It was about the size of an ordinary sheet of letter paper.

"The Northern Islander" was published at irregular intervals, especially after the close of navigation, when Beaver Island was cut off from the rest of the world. From May, 1856, until the assassination of the King two months later, the royal organ was printed as a small daily—a marvel of journalistic enterprise that surprised passengers on the boats that entered the harbor of St. James. Of the papers published at Beaver Island, Chas. J. Strang possesses but three copies, one of the weekly issues and two of the daily. Wingfield Watson, of Spring Prairie, Wis., has seventy-two of the ninety numbers of the "Islander;" his collection is believed to be the nearest to a complete file in existence. He declines to sell at any price.

The "Weekly Islander" was a newspaper of four pages, five columns to the page. The "Daily Islander" was a four-column folio, the page form being but a trifle larger than that of the "Voree Herald."

The "Herald" was devoted almost wholly to the defense of Strang's claims as leader of the Mormons. The "Islander" was conducted on the plan of a general newspaper, but devoted much space to the correspondence of traveling missionaries. A letter from George Miller mentions "settling those saints in the south that were making lumber in Wisconsin for building the temple and Nauvoo House."

The conference minutes published in the papers show that following followers of Strang, many of whom had been high dignitaries at Nauvoo, were active at Voree and St. James:

Voree—Geo. J. Adams, Wm. Marks, Gilbert Watson, Daniel Carpenter, Ebenezer Page, D. F. Botsford, Ira J. Patten, Benjamin G. Wright, Alden Hale, Roswell Packard, S. P. Bacon, Anson W. Prindle, Dennis Chidester, Jehiel Savage, Jason W. Briggs, John E. Page, Moses Smith, Lester Brooks, Samuel Bennett, Samuel Graham, Wm. Savage, Samuel E. Hull, Phineas Wright, Isaac Pierce, Nathan Wagener, John Porter, E. Whitcomb, James Blakeslee, Lorenzo Dow Hickey, Royal Tucker, P. W. Stilwell.

St. James (In addition to those prominent at Voree—John Ursbroek, Hiram G. Hall, Geo. Brownson, Edw. Preston, Walter Ostrander, John S. Comstock, C. W. Appleton, James M. Greig, E. J. More.

Besides the newspapers, the principal publications from Strang's press were these:

1. "Book of the Law of the Lord," claiming to be an inspired translation of plates discovered by Strang. First edition, 80 pages; second edition, 320 pages. Following is the wording on the title page:

The
BOOK OF THE LAW OF THE LORD
Consisting of
An Inspired Translation of Some of the Most Important Parts of the Law Given to Moses,
and a Very Few Additional Commandments, with Brief Notes and
References.
PRINTED BY COMMAND OF THE KING
AT THE ROYAL PRESS, ST. JAMES,
A. R. I.

From the preface:

"Several books are also mentioned in the Bible, but of equal authority with it, which have been lost; as for instance, another epistle of Paul to the Corinthian and the Ephesian churches, and the books of Iddo, Nathan and others, prophets of high rank in Israel.

"But of all the lost books, the most important was the Book of the Law of the Lord. This was kept in the ark of the covenant, and was held too sacred to go into the hands of strangers. When the Septuagint translation was made, the Book of the Law was kept back, and the Book lost to the Jewish nation in the time that they were subject to foreign powers. The various books in the Pentateuch, containing abstracts of some of the laws, have been read instead of it, until even the existence of the book has come to be a matter of doubt.

"It is from an authorized copy of that book, written on metallic plates, long previous to the Babylonish captivity, that this translation is made."

2. "Collection of Sacred Hymns adapted to the faith and views of the Church of Jesus Christ, of Latter-Day Saints." Voree: Gospel Press, 1850. Includes:

"Glorious things of Thee are spoken." (Zion)
"Lord, dismiss us with Thy blessing." (Dismission)
"Blest be the tie that binds." (Fraternity)
"Come, ye sinners, poor and needy." (Invitation)
"Come, let us anew, our journey pursue." (New Year's Resolve)
"Blow ye the trumpet, blow." (Gospel Trumpet)
"How form a foundation, ye saints of the Lord." (Assurance)
"Guide us, O thou great Jehovah." (Prayer)
"Lord in the morning thou shalt hear." (Morning)

The general tenor of the hymns may be gathered from following sample verses from Hymn XLV:

XLV. Book of Mormon, P. M.

1. O, who that has search'd the records of old,
   And read the last scenes of distress;
   Four and twenty were left, who with Mormon beheld,
   While their nation lay mould'ring to dust.

2. The Nephites destroyed, the Lamanites dwelt,
   For ages in sorrow unknown;
   Generations have pass'd, till the Gentiles at last,
   Have divided their lands as their own.

This is the first verse of Hymn LXXIX:

Ephraim's records, plates of gold,
Glorious things to us unfold,
Though sealed up they long have been,
To give us light they now begin.

3. "Ancient and Modern Michilimackinac, including an account of the Controversy between Mackinac and the Mormons," 1854. Reprinted by Wingfield Watson in 1894.

4. "The Diamond, being the law of Prophetic Succession and a Defense of the Calling of James J. Strang as successor to Joseph Smith, and a Full Exposition of the Law of God Touching the Succession of Prophets Holding the Presidency of the True Church, and the Proof that this Succession Has Been Kept Up." Voree, Wis., 1848.

5. "Catholic Controversy." Very scarce. I have been unable to obtain a copy.

6. "Prophetic Controversy." St. James, 1854.

VIII.

BIBLIOGRAPHY.

In addition to the Strang publications, manuscripts to which I have had access and personal letters and interviews, following printed authorities having reference to Strang have been consulted in the compilation of this paper:

"Revelations of James J. Strang," no date; compiled by Wingfield Watson.

Chapter on "Spring Prairie," in "History of Walworth County."

Chapter on Beaver Harbor Mounds, in Smithsonian annual report for 1878.

"An American Kingdom of Mormons," by F. D. Leslie, in "Magazine of Western History," April, 1886.

Chapter on "The Scattered Flock," in "Early Days of Mormonism," by J. H. Kennedy. London, 1888.

Chapter on "A New Prophet," in "The Prophet of Palmyra," by Thos. Gregg. New York, 1890.

Chapter on "Contest for the Leadership," in "Mysteries and Crimes of Mormonism," by J. H. Beadle. Philadelphia, 1870.

"The Mormons," by Lieut. J. W. Gunnison. Philadelphia, 1852.

"An American King," in "Harper's Monthly Magazine" for March, 1882.

"Beaver Island and its Mormon Kingdom," by Chas. J. Strang in the "Little Traverse Bay Souvenir." Lansing, 1895.

"History of the Traverse Region." Chicago, 1884.

"Candidates for the Pontificate," in Remy & Brenchley's "Journey to Great Salt Lake City," Vol. 1. London, 1861.

"Sketch of James Jesse Strang," in Vol. XVIII. Michigan Pioneer and Historical Collections. Lansing.

Newspaper articles consulted:

New York Tribune, July 2, 1853. (Letter from Strang defending the Beaver Island Mormons.)

New York Times, Sept. 3, 1882.

Detroit Free Press, June 30, 1889. (Statement of King Strang's assassination as witnessed by Capt. Alex. St. Barnard, of the United States steamer Michigan.)

Chicago Tribune, Oct. 2, 1892, and Oct. 13, 1895.

Detroit News, July 1, 1882.

Chicago Illustrated Journal, January, 1873.

Yenowine's Illustrated News, Milwaukee, June 24, 1888.

Milwaukee Sentinel, May 6, 1892.

· Most of the newspaper articles concerning the Beaver Island kingdom contain gross exaggerations.

www.ingramcontent.com/pod-product-compliance
Lightning Source LLC
Chambersburg PA
CBHW032044090426
42733CB00030B/649